Broken Not Shattered

Kay Nicole Varner

Broken Not Shattered

Copyright ©2014 K. Varner

All rights reserved. No part of this publication may be reproduced, distributed or transmitted in any form or by any means, including photocopying, recording, or other electronic or mechanical methods, without the prior written permission of the author, except in the case of brief quotations embodied in critical reviews and certain other noncommercial uses permitted by copyright law. For permission requests, write to the author, at the address below:

Kay Nicole Varner
P.O. Box 652
Fairburn, GA 30213

Author's Note: This is a work of fiction. Any coincidences to names, stories, or incidents are purely coincidental in nature and are of the author's ideas and creative imagination.

This book is dedicated to my sister,
"Sonya"

Your spirit of resiliency and endurance serves as a fine example of courage

It takes a great deal of bravery to stand up to our enemies

- J. K. Rowling

Preface

Broken Not Shattered is a story of abuse and resiliency spoken from the voice of Sheila: a loving wife, sister, daughter, and soon to be mother. Broken Not Shattered answers the question asked by many of why women stay in relationships when love hurts.

Sheila, like many women, was in search of love when she met Randy. The kind of love that brings about laughter in the midst of tears. The kind of love written about in fairytales little girls convince themselves will come true one day. The kind of love that makes one dance when no one else in the room can hear the music.

The moment Sheila laid eyes on Randy, she fell hard and fast. Randy was a handsome, good looking man who knew all the right words to get Sheila's attention. In the beginning, Randy was the "One" Sheila's Prince Charming.

Ultimately, Sheila's fantasy was short lived. Sheila soon discovered Randy was far from a Prince. He was more of a dangerous, frightening wolf. A wolf that was determined to mark his territory and ownership of Sheila, as well as prey on her vulnerabilities.

The more Randy's true character emerged, the more Sheila was scared to move without his permission. Randy, through a series of events and behaviors, showed Sheila with no uncertainty that he was to be feared thereby placing a hold on her like no other. Finding herself alone with no one but Randy to depend on, Sheila figured her fate was to live in hell with him *til* death do them part. Something Randy continuously recited would be the only way she would live without him.

One day something happens and Randy is imprisoned, giving Sheila a way out of the life she came to embrace as hell. Given a new lease on life, Sheila finds a way to start rebuilding and coming into a new way of living – one without restraints. Until through a series of chain events Sheila figures out, her ticket to freedom comes at a cost; one that could seal her fate forever.

Broken
Not
Shattered

{ 1 }

A man is only as good as he was raised to be
—Author Unknown

"Where do you think you are going Sheila? Huh? I said WHERE do you think you are going? I know you hear me talking to you!" Randy yelled with such force that the walls shook in fear. "You're not going to answer me? Is that it? So you are refusing to answer me?" Randy continued.

WHACK! The slap to Sheila's face came before she could brace for the strike.

"Answer me dammit!" Randy continued to demand.

I'm trying to answer. I really am but the words just won't come out. Sheila thought as she moved to ease the pain shooting from her left side, the same side where Randy, her beloved husband, just kicked her a few minutes before with the tip of his steel toe boots. The more Sheila moved and tried to shield from the hits and blows, the more Randy became enraged;

continuously tormenting her with seemingly endless kicks, slaps, and punches.

"I'm waiting for an answer Sheila! Where do you think you are going? Are you trying to leave me? Is that it? Oh so you are trying to go aren't you?" Randy insisted. "Go where? You aren't going anywhere you hear me? NOWHERE unless I say so." Randy continued to torment Sheila with his threats.

Sheila braced herself by putting her hand over her stomach as a gesture to protect her baby growing inside as she waited for the impending hit Randy was about to deliver.

"You want to leave? Here let me help you." Randy said as he grabbed a lock of Sheila's hair from the top of her head and proceeded to drag her from the living room to the bedroom by seemingly every strand of hair she had left. Once in the bedroom, Randy continued his torment by striking Sheila, alternating between his fist and hurtful kicks.

Sheila tried her best to shield the baby in her womb from Randy's madness just as she had done many other times, by turning to her side when the kicks started coming. Still, Sheila wasn't sure turning to either side would keep her little angel from being harmed, leaving Sheila to worry about the tiny jewel growing inside.

Unfortunately, the abuse Sheila endured was ongoing. Sometimes the berating came with warning, and other times like today, Randy's wrath came out of nowhere.

Sheila had hoped with the discovery of her pregnancy Randy would sustain from being physically violent towards her. Hope that now proved hopeless. Pregnancy or no pregnancy, Randy was determined to do whatever he wanted, however he wanted.

At first, for a while at least, Randy seemed happy with the idea of having a child and everything appeared to be going well. It was during this time, Sheila did not endure any hits, bruises, or threats from Randy; only occasional verbal outbursts filled with name calling. Sheila soon began to think the baby growing inside of her was a savior, her life saver, saving her from Randy's fury. However, once Sheila's abdomen started enlarging, Randy's calmness reverted and his craze reared its ugly head with a vengeance.

Now while enduring the hurtful attack, Sheila couldn't do anything but silently pray Randy would get tired and stop assaulting her. Sheila was sure if he didn't, her precious baby would not survive; especially since the last kick struck her gravely, leaving her to feel as though every organ inside was moved out of position.

The mere thought of harm coming to her baby hurt Sheila more than Randy's fury ever could. She couldn't bear the thought of any harm coming to Little Abby. That's the name Sheila wanted for her unborn jewel. *What if he hurt her? What if I've lost her too? No. No! Please God no. I can't lose her too. She's the only hope I have left.* Sheila thought as Randy kept hitting and yelling at her, commanding her to stop moving.

Sheila's thoughts were interrupted as Randy continued to shout, "Answer me! Where are you going?"

"Please Randy." Sheila pleaded, "I'm sorry. I'm so sorry. Whatever I did…. please forgive me. I….I….need to go…. the baby…."

"Go? Go where? You aren't going anywhere. Didn't you hear me the first time? Nowhere! How dare you think you are going to leave me when I am talking to you!" Randy roared.

"Randy, I'm sorry. Please…." Sheila continued to plead trying not to upset him any further.

"Stop saying you're sorry. You damn right you're sorry. Tell me something else for a change. Tell me something that will surprise me, something I don't already know. You can't can you? No I didn't think so. But I will tell you something. You make me sick! I can't stand the sight of you. I can't stand to be around you. And now you get pregnant. Why? What was your reason?" Randy blared soon pausing as to wait on Sheila to respond.

Sheila knew not to attempt to offer a response because anything she said would be used against her.

"You don't have to answer that question dear wife of mine because I already know the answer. You got pregnant so I will what….. love you? Give you the big happy family like you once had when your dad was alive? That's it right? You thought by getting pregnant, I'd be like your dad, your precious daddy that did nothing wrong. You thought by getting pregnant, you could trap me into staying with you forever. Not only are you sorry, you're stupid too. Newsflash dumbass, your little plan didn't work. Your little bastard child isn't going to make me stay. I'll go and come as I damn well please!" Randy yelled as he walked out of the bedroom towards the living area.

Seeing Randy walk away was a welcomed sight of relief for Sheila. At least for now his departure meant the blows would cease momentarily, allowing the acute pain from the latest attack to subside and giving Sheila a moment to regain herself.

    Not knowing if Randy was finished with her or not, Sheila didn't dare say a word, not even a mere whimper, nor make any moves just in case Randy made a quick u turn, then the strikes would start again. Sheila had made the mistake once before of picking herself off the floor after one of Randy's violent outbursts and paid the price of more abuse for doing so. Therefore Sheila knew to lie still and wait until the coast was truly clear.

    While waiting, Sheila could not help but to reflect on Randy's accusation of her getting pregnant on purpose. Sheila never understood his rationale especially when pregnancy tends to happen with unprotected sex, something Randy controlled not her. Sheila could recall the countless times Randy forced her to have sex, subjecting her to all kinds of humiliating, unwanted advances. Sheila did not find anything thrilling or exciting about being forced to perform degrading sexual acts. Nor did Sheila find anything exciting about being forced with threats of abuse or sometimes acts of violence if she didn't perform to his liking. Therefore, Randy's accusation of Sheila getting pregnant on purpose left her dumbfounded. Getting pregnant was the last thing Sheila thought about or attempted to do. She was too busy trying to live through the torment and torture of what Randy referred to as love making when it felt more like many have described as rape.

    Not to mention, Sheila continuously begged Randy to let her go to the doctor for her required yearly checkup and a renewal of birth control pills. Yet Randy refused to allow her to see a doctor especially after it was determined Randy had infected her with chlamydia, a sexually transmitted illness. Randy first blamed the doctor, saying the doctor's lab equipment was old and outdated. Then he accused the doctor of lying to force a wedge between him and Sheila so the doctor could have her all to himself. Eventually he blamed Sheila, accusing her of cheating. The accusation was soon followed by one method of abuse after another.

Sheila's thoughts were soon interrupted by the slamming of the front door. Finally, after what seemed like eternity, Randy was gone, at least for the time being. Sheila knew his exit was only temporary. It wasn't unusual for Randy to leave after one of his flare-ups. Sometimes he would stay away for hours; sometimes his absence was only for a few minutes. However long he stayed gone, it wasn't long enough. For Sheila wished Randy would leave and never come back.

Now if I could get up and somehow get help, Sheila thought. Not knowing how she could accomplish either task, for she hurt all over and was bleeding from unknown places.

How am I going to get help? Sheila continued to wonder. She knew getting up would be challenging but getting help was more like an impossible mission considering Sheila didn't have access to a telephone. In addition, Randy kept her locked in their tiny apartment ensuring she didn't have any contact with the outside world beyond his control. The only time Sheila was allowed out of the house is when he took her out, which wasn't very often.

The only family Sheila had was back in Colorado. Family she missed terribly, family she hadn't seen or spoken to in months. Randy made certain Sheila did not have any contact with her relatives by insisting on the move to Florida, miles away. Sheila recalled how Randy told her she didn't need to be in contact with her mom or her two sisters and how the distance was for the best because the problems between he and Sheila all centered around their constant meddling.

Actually they weren't meddling. They were trying to talk some sense into me. Sheila reflected. *Somehow, they knew Randy was a bad seed. Somehow they knew.*

A sudden sharp pain in her stomach brought Sheila back to the matter at hand. Sheila realized she had to figure out a way to get help because if she didn't she was sure to die; if not today, then one day, and perhaps soon. Sheila could tell the beatings were getting worse every sense the change of attitude came about the baby. Randy no longer wanted the child. Therefore, he was determined to beat the baby out of her.

As the sharp pain started to grow in intensity, Sheila acknowledged she had to find the strength to get up some way, somehow. She just had to. Encouraging her weakened legs to hold her up, Sheila managed to make it to the bathroom with the help of the walls which she used to hold herself in an upright position.

In view of the mirror, Sheila could barely make out the image of the face, her face, staring back at her. Her lips were swollen to the size of an orange. Her nose and cheeks were covered in blood. Her left eye was closed shut and her right eye was discolored with some variation of the color purple. Seeing her reflection brought tears to Sheila's eyes. Just as the tears started to trickle down her face in a steady stream, Sheila felt something wet flowing down her legs. *Oh no! No! This can't be.* She thought in panic, quickly making it to the commode and hurriedly pulling down her underwear.

Not seeing any evidence of blood signaling harm to her unborn baby, Sheila sighed in relief. The wetness was evidently from her bladder being full and starting to release on its own Sheila concluded.

Sheila sat on the commode for a while thinking of what to do next. She was weak, tired, and ached all over. As Sheila sat contemplating on what to do, her thoughts were suddenly interrupted by a forceful knock at the front door.

Hearing the knock at the door made Sheila uneasy. Randy always told her to never go near the door or window. Her orders were to stay in the room and go no farther than the kitchen. Orders Sheila knew to obey. Once while cleaning, Sheila went into the room Randy called his study to straighten up. Randy came home, saw his desk organized and instead of being happy, he went ballistic. Organizing his desk earned Sheila a fist to her left eye, the one eye Randy seemed to favor the most. Since then Sheila only went into the rooms where she was permitted.

For this reason, Sheila continued to ignore the commanding knocks. However, the banging soon grew louder and more persistent. Sheila then heard a male voice state, "Ms.....Ms. are you in there? Open up it's the police."

The police? Why would the police be outside the door? Sheila wondered. The more she tried to ignore the persistence of the knocks, the louder they became. Sheila grew nervous. She knew she couldn't open the door even if she wanted to because she didn't have a key to the deadbolt lock. Besides, Sheila wasn't even sure it was the police. *What if it were Randy pretending to be the police just to see if I would be disobedient and open the door? But what if it is really the police?* Sheila speculated silently.

Curiosity getting the best of her, Sheila arose from the commode and proceeded to walk to the front door to look through the peephole. Somehow this plan was better played out in her head, for the next thing Sheila knew her legs refused to support her anymore as she fell hard and fast onto the floor.

{ 2 }

Revelation

"Miss. Miss? Hi there. I'm Dr. Walker. Can you hear me?"

Startled by the unfamiliar voice and strange surroundings, Sheila didn't respond but proceeded to stare at the strange looking man in a white coat talking to her.

Who was he? Where was she? What is that annoying beeping noise and where is it coming from? Sheila thought as she tried to make sense of the environment. Looking around the room, Sheila could tell she wasn't in the apartment she and Randy shared. She appeared to be in a hospital.

Sheila attempted to look around the room for a familiar face but found it difficult to see clearly. Everything was blurry in her right eye and she couldn't see anything out of the left one. As Sheila began to panic, one of the machines she was connected to starting hysterically making a loud chiming sound. Just then a nurse named Jenny came in, asking Sheila to calm down and proceeded to explain to Sheila that she was in an ICU unit at Memorial Hospital.

"Memorial Hospital? What? Why? How?" Sheila managed to mumble. Then it hit her. The baby. Her Abby. Something must have happened. Sheila closed her eyes trying to remember how she ended up in the hospital but couldn't. The more she tried, the more she kept drawing a blank. Sheila lifted her weak hand and placed it on her stomach while opening her eyes in an attempt to see the nurse and asked, "My baby?"

Nurse Jenny responded by putting her head down as Dr. Walker interrupted saying, "I'm sorry," bringing to light Sheila's worse nightmare. All hope, her hope was gone. The pain Sheila now felt was worse than anything Randy ever did to her including beating her unconscious.

Just as Nurse Jenny offered comfort, Officer Jennings approached the bed introducing himself.

"Hi ma'am. I'm Detective Jennings with the Bean County Police Department. I would like to ask you a few questions." He said sternly.

Ask me questions? Sheila thought as she wondered what was going on.

Detective Jennings continued. "Can you tell me what happened to you at your residence?"

Sheila was stunned and no longer cared what happened or why. It didn't matter. Nothing mattered. She was alone, all alone.

"Ms. Mathis? What happened on Thursday?" Office Jennings asked. His tone indicated he was running out of patience.

"Thursday? What day is today?" Sheila managed to get out as the tears streamed steadily down her face.

"It's Sunday. Now tell me what happened ma'am?" Officer Jennings asked again.

"I'm not sure officer. I don't know how I ended up in the hospital." Sheila responded.

"I can fill you in on how you got here," Officer Jennings responded. "But I need you to tell me what caused you to come here okay?" Officer Jennings stated and asked at the same time. Once Sheila nodded in agreement for the exchange of information to take place, Office Jennings continued.

"A police unit was dispatched to your residence due to a domestic disturbance call made by one of your neighbors. The officers knocked for quite some time and were about to leave until they heard a sudden loud clack and scream coming from your apartment. Following protocol, they gained entry into your residence and found you passed out on the floor from an apparent fall. Emergency services were dispatched; you were then transported to the hospital. Dr. Walker can fill you in on the rest from that point." Officer Jennings concluded.

"Well that explains what happened." Sheila acknowledged under her breath not realizing Officer Jennings or anyone else heard her.

"Not exactly ma'am. See the fall you took explains the gash on your head and perhaps the bruise to your arm. It doesn't explain the multiple injuries to your face, the internal bleeding, and broken ribs. That's why I'm here. I need you to tell me what happened to you before the fall. Who did this to you?" Officer Jennings asked again.

Sheila turned her head in shame. It's not that she didn't want to answer the officer, she didn't know how. How does one admit to others, especially strangers, one's weakness, fear, and shame of abuse? The mere thought was humiliating. Sheila couldn't. She just couldn't admit such embarrassment. She didn't even know where to begin even if she wanted to.

Silence grew in the room as Sheila offered no response to the officer. Finally, Nurse Jenny sat down beside Sheila's bed, grabbed her hand and said, "It's ok. I understand. I've been there."

Sheila turned her head to look at Jenny with amazement as she thought, *there is no way this woman understands. She wouldn't be so weak and allow a man to hit her, demean her, or humiliate her. No. She can't understand. Jenny obviously thinks something else happened. Yes that's it. She thinks my injuries are from the fall.*

Nurse Jenny still holding Sheila's hand gave it a squeeze and said, "My ex-boyfriend favored my right eye. That's the one he hit the most."

Sheila gasped in disbelief. *Was she hearing correctly? Did Jenny truly understand?*

"Ms. Mathis or can I call you Sheila?" Jenny continued.

Sheila nodded yes.

"Although our stories differ somewhat, I am very familiar with feelings of shame and fear. What you must understand is if you want the abuse to stop, you have to let us help you. Please. I know you are scared. I can only imagine your terror. But please let us help. Okay?" Jenny pleaded compassionately.

Sheila again nodded yes.

"Who did this to you?" Jenny asked tenderly.

Sheila closed her eyes knowing her response could change her life for the better or maybe even the worse.

Considering she had nothing more to lose because she had lost everything already, Sheila responded "Randy."

{ 3 }

Home Sweet Home

It had been five months since her discharge from Memorial Hospital. A long five months filled with counseling, support groups, physical therapy, and above all, questions. Questions from everyone: her family, the police, the doctors, the counselors, the pastor, old friends.

This journey or road to recovery wasn't proving to be an easy one. Sheila had to adapt to living in the real world again; One that consisted of her being able to answer the phone, talking to people, expressing her feelings, etc.. Things she hadn't done in such a long time. Although she was back in Colorado with her mom and sisters, Sheila had not grown comfortable in her surroundings. She looked over her shoulder everywhere she went as well as continued to be haunted by nightmares of Randy coming after her every time she closed her eyes. The psychiatrist prescribed her something to help her sleep which helped some nights. Yet other nights, the medicine seemed to make the dreams more vivid and real.

The psychiatrist concluded the nightmares would soon appear less as she relaxed in her new life and would eventually stop all together once the trauma was behind her. The problem was no one knew when Sheila's frightful Randy chapter would be over. The District Attorney told Sheila, she would have to come back to Florida to testify against Randy and she would be notified of the trial date. Luckily, Randy had outstanding warrants for other criminal acts in other states that Sheila knew nothing about, so her case was to be tried at a later time, one that she was promised to get advanced notice about. In the meantime, Sheila looked online every day at the Bean County inmate database where Randy was being held, making sure he was still locked away, far from her.

"Sheila, sweetheart do you want pickles on your burger or not?" Sheila's thoughts were interrupted by Carol, her middle sister.

"No. No pickles," Sheila answered.

Being at home with her mom and sisters was something Sheila never imagined she would live to see. Ironically, the fall that took her life also saved it. Had Sheila not fallen, none of this would be happening. She wouldn't be back in Colorado with her family, sitting on the back patio watching her nieces play, and Randy would not be in jail awaiting trial.

Sheila's mom, Theresa, was a pillar of strength. After receiving a call from the hospital, Theresa immediately made her way to Florida to be by Sheila's side. The reunion brought tears of relief for both mother and child. So much so, the nurse on duty had to calm both women down particularly Theresa. Theresa later explained her excitement was due to being overwhelmed with joy with the discovery of Sheila not only being alive but surviving a horrid beating that left her unrecognizable.

Even after hearing the gory details of what had occurred in Sheila's life nothing was said, no judgment or I told you so. Theresa's response was quite the opposite. She held Sheila and cried silently, apologizing for Sheila's pain as if it were her fault.

Surprisingly, Sheila's sister Melissa also had nothing to say. Which was unusual because Melissa always had plenty to say, especially when it came to other people and what they should or shouldn't be doing. Sheila's sister Carol was vocal in verbalizing her great desire to beat Randy's you know what, like he beat Sheila's. Actually, she expressed wanting to do a lot more. Carol always had a horrifying way of thinking even as an adolescent. It's a wonder how she ended up being a lawyer instead of needing one.

Sheila's wounds were healing quite nicely on the outside, the swelling had gone down to the point there wasn't any evidence of the violence she endured. The bruises to her face had disappeared and her vision to her left eye was improving.

Yes, the outside was on the road to recovery; but the inside was a different story. Sheila may have escaped the physical torture of Randy but the mental and emotional damage was far from over. Sheila still wept over the loss of her baby girl. She was nineteen weeks pregnant when the loss occurred. According to Dr. Walker, it was hard to say if the fall caused the final demise or Randy's abuse. That's what he told Detective Jennings anyway when asked.

{ 4 }

Reflections

Sheila's constant nightmares consisted of Randy chasing and attacking her, or baby Abby crying out for help. The dreams often caused Sheila to cry out in the middle of the night. Sometimes the cries were so loud that Theresa, Carol, or Melissa would wake her and stay to comfort her. With Theresa working the night shift, Carol and Melissa were forced to take turns watching over Sheila, never leaving her alone. Sheila couldn't even go to the store by herself.

Sheila knew eventually she would have to address the constant monitoring. For it was time for her to start getting her life back on track and looking for a job was on top of her list now that the doctor had cleared her to do so.

Sheila looked forward to working again. She hoped having something other than her past to focus on would help jumpstart the process of healing. Which would ultimately, allow her to feel alive once more. Although Sheila desired to get back in the workforce and gain some sort of independence, she knew finding a job wouldn't be easy.

When Sheila married Randy, she was in her third year of teaching as a first grade educator. Sheila loved her job and it showed. In no time, she won teacher of the year and was rumored to be up for promotion to lead grade level coordinator. Unfortunately, Randy made sure Sheila didn't advance by deliberately jeopardizing her position with constant phone calls and loud harassing outbursts filled with accusations of one thing after another; outbursts that frequently occurred right in the middle of the school lobby.

His actions were so bad that one day Sheila was called in by her principal, whom she respected, who reluctantly informed her that if she didn't get rid of

Randy, the school would have no other choice but to let her take some time off to get her life together.

    Little did anyone know, getting rid of Randy seemed impossible for Sheila to do. Sheila had left Randy numerous times only to be wooed back by empty promises and guilt-filled apologies that faded faster than they came. Eventually, even Randy couldn't fake the tears of sorrow after one of his rages and started using other tactics to control her. Tactics such as threatening to harm her children, the kids she taught, as well as her nieces and her mom if she ever left him.

    Randy knew he could control Sheila with threats. He knew she was close to her family and loved her job dearly. Sheila couldn't bear the thought of Randy making good on his promises especially after she figured out he had sabotaged Theresa's car one day.

    Theresa was on her way home from work when her car suddenly starting jerking and making funny noises. Somehow, Theresa managed to make it to a nearby convenience store where she called for automobile tow assistance. Fighting past her fatigue, Theresa had the tow driver take the car to Mr. Greene's Auto Shop for analysis. To Theresa's surprise, her car was out of oil. Strangely, the mechanics could not find any evidence of a leak and Theresa denied seeing the oil light warning indicator that usually comes on when the oil is getting low. This puzzled everyone that heard about this yet no one would have guessed Randy was the culprit; no one that is except Sheila.

It was later discovered, Randy had taken the oil out of Theresa's car so she would be stranded on her way to work not from work. Sheila, to this day, doesn't know exactly what Randy was going to do to Theresa if the car would have stopped like he figured but she did know it wasn't anything good.

When Sheila found out about her mom's car trouble, it didn't take long for Sheila to figure out Randy had something to do with it. Although he hadn't confessed at the time, she knew. Why else would Randy ask her if the mechanics were able to save her mom's car when Sheila herself didn't know something was wrong? And her suspicions were later validated when she tried to leave Randy for good prior to the move to Florida. He told her in no uncertain terms was he leaving her alone and would see to it to that she would forever suffer if she left him.

His exact words that day were, "I sure would hate for something to happen to your beloved mom especially after that car incident. Just think what could have happened to her if her car would have died while she was driving to work especially since she likes to take all those shortcuts on those back roads."

Sheila didn't need any convincing after that. She packed her things and moved with Randy far away from her family in order to protect them.

***

Reminiscing made Sheila uncomfortable. Somehow talking or even thinking about her life with Randy brought back feelings of pain. Pain Sheila desired to forget. Desiring to forget was easy, doing so was not.

Haunted by the fears of yesterday, Sheila was determined to regain control of her life and getting a job was an intricate part of this goal.

"Sheila. Sheila? Do you want to go with Carol on Friday?" Sheila heard Theresa ask.

"What? Go where?" Sheila responded.

"To your cousin Francine's bachelorette party? It may be fun to hang out and let your hair down. You know have some fun." Carol chimed in.

"No. I don't think so. I'm not ready to go out like that yet." Sheila answered.

"Well, I'll just let Tony, my supervisor, know I can't work on Friday. That way Carol, you can go to the celebration." Theresa stated.

"I can cancel my plans mom. Mark and I can reschedule our trip and go another time." Melissa expressed.

"None of you will change any of your plans. I am more than capable of staying by myself." Sheila exclaimed.

With this statement, the women all fell quiet, which was a rare event for the Thompson family. Just as Theresa spoke to interject, Sheila pleaded for the opportunity to prove to them she was ready for independence. Listening to her family go back and forth as to who would cancel their plans to literally babysit her was more than enough reason for Sheila to take the opportunity to prove to everyone she was self-sufficient. Sheila knew she had to make the first step in gaining some sort of normalcy in getting her life back or at least start living, and not just merely existing.

The rest of the evening was filled with hints of fear - fear of the unknown. The Thompson women checked the locks on the windows and doors. Mark, Melissa's husband, tested the alarm making sure all the contacts and sirens worked.

Fearful or not, Sheila knew she had to try. She had to make more than mere baby steps to get closer to her goal. She needed to take a giant leap; a leap that consisted of finding gainful employment and being her own babysitter.

Mind Games

Sheila had emailed multiple resumes within the past couple of weeks, being careful to avoid any teaching positions. Yet out of all the resumes she sent out, she had not received any responses. Melissa suggested Sheila go back into education. Although, Sheila desired a job she wasn't ready to be responsible for anyone else's child especially when she proved she couldn't safe guard her own.

Perhaps if I dressed the part and walked into various places advertising needing help, I would have a better chance of getting hired. Sheila thought. So bright and early Monday morning, Sheila left her seemingly safe haven in pursuit of employment. The theory of going from place to place to better the chances of finding a job proved to be just that – A Theory. By the end of the day, Sheila had visited at least ten different bank branches, multiple department stores, and other specialty stores with promises of callbacks. Tuesday ended up being a repeat of Monday and by the end of the week, Sheila figured out her path to re-inventing herself was not going to be an easy one.

By Friday evening Sheila was exhausted from the endless job searching. She looked forward to relaxing and curling up with a good book, something funny or perhaps a romantic novel.

Theresa lingered around trying to find an excuse, any excuse to stay home from work, while Melissa and Carol both called numerous times offering to rearrange their plans. Sheila insisted to all she would be fine and encouraged each to go about their activities.

Finding herself alone on a Friday night, brought on feelings of worry and glee at the same time for Sheila. Sheila had gotten relaxed with the false sense of security of having her family constantly around her. She had grown comfortable with the notion that as long as someone was around to protect her, the less of a chance Randy had to come after or attack her.

Although Sheila knew Randy was physically in Florida sitting in a jail cell, her thoughts continuously convinced her Randy was near watching her every move and just waiting for the right moment to launch his attack.

As Sheila found herself alone, she felt somewhat afraid but refused to allow fear to get the best of her. *I can do this.* Sheila coaxed herself. *I can survive. I will survive.* This coaxing proved to be a beneficial exercise, one she frequently found herself using through the course of the night.

As Sheila lay on the couch, she tried reading a book called *RainFalls So Your Light Can Shine.* A book Theresa recommended about the power of love and forgiveness but every noise, or subtle squeak the house created terrified Sheila, making her jump in response. So much so, Sheila knew reading was not going to work out while she was home all alone. Sheila then tried drawing, something that usually brought her peace, but found it hard to concentrate with her mind being filled with thoughts of fear.

Sheila then turned on the television hoping to find something intriguing and interesting enough to entertain her mind and keep it from looming in fear. After flipping through numerous channels, she eventually found a cute love story about two strangers meeting on the subway and falling for one another. Love was something Sheila desired. Love was something Sheila believed in and found herself daydreaming she was the lady on the subway meeting Mr. Right.

At some point Sheila must have drifted off to sleep for she was soon awakened by the sight of Randy smiling as he stroked her forehead while saying "Hello beautiful."

At first, Sheila couldn't move. She couldn't believe it. *Was Randy really here with her? How? When?* Sheila didn't know what to do but she knew she had to do something. She had to at least try to get away from him. Sheila quickly attempted to move but the more she tried to move to fight him off and stop him from touching her, the more he smiled at her as his touch grew harder and more persistent.

Oh no, he is going to kill me. Sheila thought. Sheila knew it was only one thing she could do to try to stay alive and that was to fight with all her might.

Sheila started screaming and swinging her arms and legs hysterically. Yet the more she swung, the more it felt as though she was hitting nothing but air.

Exhausted, Sheila decided to accept her fate and face defeat. She quit fighting, knowing Randy would thrush into attack, this time finishing the job he didn't complete back in their tiny apartment in Florida.

Sheila braced herself for the inevitable; praying Randy would be finished with her and be gone before her mom or sisters came home.

***

"Sheila? Sheila? Honey wake up? You're shaking and sweaty? What's going on? What's wrong?" Carol asked in worry.

Sheila jumped at the sound of Carol's voice. "Carol. Oh Carol! Thank God you are here. Wait a minute, is he gone? Are you okay?" Sheila inquired in panic.

"Of course I'm okay. What are you talking about? Who is he?" Carol asked perplexed.

"Randy….. Carol he came. Carol he was here. I tried to fight him. I did, I really did but I couldn't seem to hit him. The more I tried, the more I couldn't….I…I never made the target." Sheila said ruffled.

"Sweetie you just had a dream, a very bad dream. See you're fine. No one is here. No one has been here." Carol offered empathetically.

"No Carol. I'm telling you he was here. He touched me. He spoke to me. He came to kill me. You have to believe me. He was here!" Sheila cried out trying to convince Carol she wasn't imagining anything.

"Sheila when I came home the door was locked and the alarm was on. Honey if it makes you feel any better, I will call the police." Carol offered.

"Yes call the police. Carol I know he was here. I just know it," Sheila said convincingly.

Promptly Carol picked up the phone and called the local authorities. Within minutes, two uniform officers were there to investigate. They checked all the windows and doors which were locked and reported nothing seemed out of order.

During this time, Carol checked on the Bean County Police Department website to check to see if Randy was still in lockup and saw that he was. The puzzled officers took a statement and left. Meanwhile, Theresa had arrived home from work nervous and full of worry.

Sheila felt more confused than ever. She must have been dreaming after all. Yet, somehow the dream felt real and was different from any of the other nightmares. Sheila sat dazed in silence as Carol held her hand and Theresa double checked the latches on the windows as well as the locks on the doors. When Sheila finally spoke, she softly said, "I'm sorry."

"Sorry for what dear? You have nothing to be sorry about," Carol said gently.

"I must have fallen asleep and had a nightmare causing all this commotion. I got everyone revved up over a dream. I'm sorry. I'm so sorry. I really proved my readiness for independence didn't I? I guess I'm not as ready as I thought." Sheila said with embarrassment.

"Sheila, you have been through a lot. The abuse you endured didn't happen overnight so the healing sure isn't going to occur in one night. The healing process takes time. Eventually, you will get there." Theresa said as she cried while holding Sheila in her arms.

"What if I never get there?" Sheila responded through the tears.

"You will." Theresa spoke calmly as she kissed Sheila on the forehead.

"Mom, how can you be so sure?"

"Because you are a fighter who has the desire to live. You proved that while in the hospital months ago and again tonight." Theresa answered undoubtedly.

"I proved nothing tonight but how scared and paranoid I am." Sheila sighed.

"On the contrary my dear, the dream you had was real. The events in the dream were real and when faced with the threat of death, you were determined to fight to the end. I have no doubt you will win this battle. No doubt at all." Theresa stated boldly.

Sheila grew silent not sure if this battle could be won and if so, would she survive. Accepting the occurrence of the evening was a dream, Sheila realized she had a long road ahead of her for the realness of the illusion proved she was still powerless and defenseless when it came to Randy. One thing for sure, had the horror of Randy's comeback been authentic, Sheila would have lost the fight. The fight needed to save her life.

{ 6 }

Guarded

It had been two weeks since the embarrassing delusion of fear and everyone was on high alert. Theresa with the help of Carol and Melissa, formulated a spreadsheet indicating days and times of who would stay with Sheila making sure she was never left alone not even for a second.

Melissa accompanied Sheila to the store or on job interviews. Carol practically moved in full-time to be with her, while Teresa kept a close eye whenever possible. If any of the three ladies were unable to cover, Melissa's husband, Mark, had to stand guard. At no uncertain time was Sheila left alone, unless she went to the restroom. Even then if she was in there too long, someone was coming to check on her.

Sheila knew all this attention was not conducive to her meeting her goal of independence. "I may have had a setback but I have to keep trying," Sheila pleaded with her family when a conflict in the watch scheduling occurred. Although the family agreed with Sheila, her pleas were ignored.

Sheila was growing weary of not having any employment prospects and being guarded in a makeshift witness protection program. So much so she was contemplating going back to school and majoring in anything that would give her five minutes to herself.

Finally, Sheila's silent prayers were answered when she received a call from Mackee Taylor & Moss Law firm offering her an administrative assistant position she had interviewed for over a month ago.

Sheila was shocked she was offered the job because she lacked law experience but met all the other qualifications. She recalled Ms. Whyte, the hiring Human Resources Director, stating the firm was interested in hiring someone with a strong legal background but promised to be in touch if another position opened that lined up with Sheila's qualifications.

Sheila, thrilled to receive the call from Ms. Whyte, gladly accepted the position without hesitation when the offer was made.

{ 7 }

Developments

Being back in the workforce felt exhilarating. Sheila couldn't believe how fast she was able to catch on in her new work environment. Before long, she was performing as if she had been there for years. More so than ever, Sheila was determined to get her life back on track.

It took a while for her family to adapt to her job and the long hours associated with it. Sheila's work hours were 9-5 on paper but working for a major law firm, everyone soon realized the stated hours were more of an ideal than reality. Sometimes, Sheila left before five but most times Sheila worked until seven or eight at night including tonight. Thankfully, today was Friday, which brought a feeling of relief for Sheila.

The weekends were a welcomed joy for Sheila because they allowed her to catch up on her hobby of drawing. Sheila loved to sketch anything – the skyline at sunrise; the trees as they bloomed signifying spring was near; or the children as they played innocently with one another. Drawing helped Sheila's mind to relax which allowed her to rest peacefully, something Sheila looked forward to doing without the constant interruption of unwanted nightmares.

Sheila also looked forward to spending time with family, something the weekends allowed to happen because that's when everyone's schedule permitted their togetherness to occur. Spending time together seemed to help ease everyone's tension, especially Theresa's.

Sheila was starting to feel like her old self, pre Randy; confident and lively. Although Sheila still was plagued with memories that often presented themselves as nightmares from time to time, she was taking things day by day and today was a good day.

By eight o'clock, Sheila figured it was time to call it quits. She had completed all reports and even formulated her to do list for Monday. Sheila shut down her computer and waved goodbye to her office mate, Sarah, who looked like she was nowhere near leaving any time soon.

On her way to the elevator, Sheila forgot she hadn't called downstairs to request a security escort to her car. Theresa made Sheila promise to do this every day no matter what time she left. Thinking of the promise she made, Sheila knew she better find a phone. Not that she felt she was in danger but Sheila hadn't yet gotten comfortable with her new found freedom.

Security guard Peterson met her at the garage entrance to walk her to her car. Sheila wasn't sure how much help this guard would be if she were in danger because he wasn't armed with any type of defense weapon. Sure there were armed guards in the building but the armed officers were not assigned to car escort duty unless they were providing escort service to one of the law partners.

As Security Guard Peterson walked Sheila to her car, which was parked three rows from the garage entrance, they spoke about any weekend plans and how good it felt to be off for the next two days.

As Sheila approached her car, she noticed something was wrong.

"Looks like you have a couple of flat tires." She heard Mr. Peterson say.

"I see." replied Sheila. "I better call the automobile association."

With both front tires being flat, her anticipation to get home had to be put off just a little while longer.

***

Sheila finally arrived at her residence a little before eleven p.m. The tow truck driver was kind enough to drop her car off to the Mr. Greene's Auto Shop. Mr. Greene, the owner, assured her - her car would be ready by noon on Saturday. The driver then brought her home where Carol, Mark, and Melissa were anxiously waiting for her arrival.

Walking up the driveway towards the front door, Sheila got a weird feeling of nervousness in the pit of her stomach. Suddenly, she heard a rustling noise coming from the bush near the fenced area that surrounded the back yard. Sheila turned towards the noise just as the front door swung open.

"Oh thank God, you're okay," Carol blurted as she ran towards Sheila hugging her tightly.

"Of course I'm okay. Why wouldn't I be?" Sheila asked already knowing the answer.

Ignoring Sheila's remark, Carol continued. "How did you manage to flatten two tires?"

"I don't know. The tow driver speculated I had nails in the tires causing them to be flattened. I'll know more tomorrow after Mr. Greene gets me back up and running again." Sheila stated as she paused from following Carol into the house.

"Sheila, is something wrong?" Carol asked.

"No, I thought I heard a creepy rustling noise coming from near the bushes by the fence." Sheila responded in curiosity.

"Let me make sure I understand. You think you heard a creepy noise yet you questioned me as to why I would be concerned about your well-being." Carol smirked.

"OKAY wrong choice of words." Sheila chuckled as they both went inside, closing the front door.

Just then the phone rang. It was Theresa worried sick because no one had called her to let her know Sheila had made it home safely. Theresa let everyone know how displeased she was not to have been notified right away of Sheila's arrival home.

Sheila understood Theresa's worry. Sheila also understood her family had reason to panic but the amount of check in phone calls and constant over-excitement made it hard for Sheila to feel or gain a sense of normalcy. This was something she tried explaining to them but no one seemed to understand why she felt this way. Sheila was grateful for everything her mom and sisters had done for her and continued to do for her, therefore, she didn't put up a fight or get upset demanding a change come sooner rather than later.

On Saturday, Mr. Greene called a little after noon informing Sheila her car was ready. Sheila was eager to pick up her car and get home for the sooner she did so, the sooner her weekend could truly begin.

As Theresa and Sheila made their way to pick up Sheila's car, which was actually Theresa's old car, Sheila couldn't help but notice the fatigue written all over Theresa's face. She also noticed, Theresa looked pale and had lost weight.

"Mom, are you ok?" Sheila asked.

"I'm just fine." Theresa answered. "Why do you ask?"

"You look tired." Sheila responded.

"I am a bit tired. I didn't get a lot of sleep this morning after I got off work." Theresa stated.

Sheila wasn't convinced Theresa's presentation stemmed from only one sleepless morning; especially when the look of worry was written all over her face.

Strange Times

Mr. Greene was an elderly gentleman who was well known in the neighborhood. He was an honest business man if one ever existed and was well respected by everyone. As the two women parked and approached the entrance to the shop, they were greeted by Mr. Greene, himself. Mr. Greene wasted no time in going over the problem and explanation of the charges.

"We didn't have to replace either tire so in actuality you don't owe me anything." He said.

"So you mean you were able to fix both tires?" Theresa asked.

"Well I guess you can call it that. Sheila, you clearly had two flat tires when the car was brought in. I figured you must have run over a nail or something. Strange thing is, neither Ted nor I, could find a hole in either tire. Not one. We searched and searched but couldn't find anything. No nail, no screw, no cut, no leak. Nothing. Somehow the air just went out of the tires. Sometimes strange things happen that can't be explained and this is one of those times." Mr. Greene concluded.

Sheila heard Mr. Greene but wasn't sure she understood him. How was it possible for both front tires to be totally flat and the cause not found by trained individuals? Sheila couldn't believe what she was hearing. Better yet, she didn't know what to think.

Before she let paranoia set in, she thanked Mr. Greene and proceeded to drive home never once making eye contact with Theresa. Sheila didn't know what happened to cause her tires to go flat but what she did know was Theresa's worry was about to heighten even more, if that was possible.

{ 9 }

Unsoundness Unfolds

It had been a week since the incident and things in the Thompson household had gotten worse since the flat tire occurrence. Everyone, more so Theresa had become obsessed with the protection of Sheila patrol. Theresa insisted on Sheila being dropped off and picked up from work whenever possible. When this was not feasible due to conflicting schedules, Mark was sucked into stopping by every morning in route to work to check the tires on Sheila's car.

By the following Saturday, Sheila had decided it was time to address the over protection duty because everyone's paranoia was making her feel nervous, really nervous. *What better time to address the family than at the weekly planned gathering that occurred every Saturday where everyone agreed to their watch over me schedules.* Sheila thought.

Like clockwork, Mark started the grill. Theresa started giving orders to Melissa and Sheila on how to clean and season the steaks as well as prepare the corn on the cob for grilling. Carol was in charge of the salad and beverages. The kids were busy playing and not paying any attention to what the grownups were up to.

"Don't forget to marinate the steak with the rub I bought from the market." Theresa yelled to Melissa and Sheila.

"I think we are out of the steak marinade mom." Sheila answered.

"Sheila's right. We must have used the last little bit when we had steaks before." Melissa chimed in.

"We have to have something to season the steaks with besides plain salt and pepper." Theresa replied.

"Melissa, do we have garlic cloves, teriyaki or Worcestershire sauce, seasoned salt, and Dijon mustard?" Teresa asked while walking indoors to look for the needed supplies herself.

"Looks like we have everything except for the sauce. Hmmm…. seems like a store run is calling. Do we need anything else from the market while I'm going?" Theresa asked.

"Grab some more mayo for the macaroni salad, just in case." Carol called out.

Theresa grabbed her purse and headed towards the door. She soon doubled back as she remembered Sheila parked behind her in the driveway, blocking her in.

"Sheila, dear where are your keys? Your car is the only one not blocked in by anyone." Theresa asked.

"They are where the usually are, on the table." Sheila answered.

Theresa looked on the table in the fruit bowl where Sheila usually placed the keys but couldn't find them. "No, I don't see them. Where else could they be?" Theresa called out.

Sheila thought for a minute, trying to recap her steps from last night after arriving home. "Maybe they're on my nightstand by my cell phone," Sheila stated attempting to recall where the keys could be.

"Nope, not there either," Theresa said wearily.

Soon the entire household stopped what they were doing to look for the missing keys. The kids took joy in the hide and seek key game. Still nothing. The keys were nowhere to be found - not in Sheila's purse, not in the kitchen, not locked in the car, not in the dining area, bathroom, or back patio. Nowhere.

"We know they are here somewhere, let's take a break and check the places we have already looked. Perhaps we overlooked them the first time." Carol said while looking at Sheila attempting to comfort her worry.

After an exhausting search, the team decided it was too late for steaks and decided to order pizza for dinner instead.

One hour later, the door bell rung.

"The pizza is here. The pizza is here!" Little Carly, Sheila's niece, called out in excitement.

Mark went to the door to pay for the pizzas. As he opened the door anticipating a quick money and pizza exchange, the driver asked, "Did any one lose these keys? I found them outside in the driveway."

***

Sheila was relieved and puzzled by the finding of the missing keys. There were so many questions going on inside her head making her weary of the seemingly constant puzzling coincidences. First the dream, then the flat tires, followed by the rustling noise coming from the bushes, now the keys.

Are all these incidences purely coincidental in nature? Am I losing my mind from the fear and paranoia? Or is Randy behind the unexplained chance happenings? Sheila wondered. There was only one way to find out. Sheila knew it was time to face her fears and call the Florida District Attorney directly for a status on her case and above all make sure Randy was still in jail.

Sunday the family gathered for the weekly meeting minus the kids. They were on play dates with Mark's sister. With the kids being away there wasn't a lot of chatter going on.

As everyone sat down Theresa started her normal speech which ended with everyone agreeing to their weekly assignments

Sheila couldn't help but notice Theresa's health was declining. Theresa was easily fatigued and recently had to increase her blood pressure medication. Sheila's eyes filled with tears because she felt responsible for her mom's worry. As happy as Sheila was to be back with her family, she couldn't bear the thought of causing affliction to the woman she loved the most in this world - her mom.

Carol was the first to speak after the assignments were settled. "I think we can all agree we have had some unusual things to occur within the past couple of weeks."

Heads nodded in agreement.

"I think the overzealousness is making us all paranoid." Carol continued, "No matter what, we are all in this together."

Everyone agreed and bid farewell for the evening. Sheila's eyes filled with tears.

Monday morning seem to come too soon. Sheila was fatigued from all the stress and apprehension. She thought about calling out sick for a much needed day of mental and emotional rest but Monday's were the busiest day in the office due to the new cases presented from the weekend mayhem. Sheila was amazed at what the rich and famous got themselves into and were willing to pay big money to get out of.

{ 10 }

The Product of Thoughts

This Monday was no exception. The phones started ringing from the moment they were taken off of the answering service and every lawyer had a new agenda to work on. Sheila kept looking at the clock hoping things would calm down at some point so she could make the call to District Attorney Mr. Crain's office. Finally at about three o'clock in the afternoon, calmness settled in. Sheila took a break to find a quiet space where she wouldn't be interrupted.

As she dialed the number found on the card given to her while she was still in the hospital, Sheila could feel every muscle in her body tense, while her heart raced in anxiety. Soon she was connected to Mr. Crain's assistant, Danny Reeder. Sheila explained the nature of her call. Mr. Reeder took her information and promised to find out some data and assured her that he would be in touch with the information she requested as soon as possible.

As the day neared to an end, Sheila figured out, their definition of as soon as possible didn't quite match her emergency status. Deciding to call it quits, Sheila waited in the lobby for her Monday night escort home to arrive - Carol.

On the ride home, Carol noticed Sheila wasn't her normally talkative self. Usually, Sheila couldn't wait to tell her about her day. This time though, Sheila rode in silence.

Carol, along with Melissa and Mark, were growing worried about both Sheila and Theresa. Both looked frail and neither one had said much since the key incident.

Carol decided to continue to ride in silence and leave Sheila alone in her thoughts. Carol could only imagine what was going through Sheila's mind especially with all she had endured in the past.

Being a defense attorney, Carol felt Sheila's anxiety was warranted. Carol knew criminals had a way of tormenting their victims, even while behind bars. Usually they got a fellow inmate, friend, or relative to do their dirty work. Sheila didn't know this but Carol had already put fillers out through some of her contacts to try to find out who Randy might have gotten to get to Sheila. Carol was hopeful her sources would pan out and she could put a stop to this craziness without Sheila knowing what was going on. So far her sources had not been able to come up with anything.

The drive home seemed to take longer than usual. Sheila wanted to do nothing but lie in bed and cry herself to sleep. Sheila hoped she could get a good's night rest without any dreams. Lately, the nightmares were appearing less and less as the psychiatrist predicted. Perhaps because reality was scary enough Sheila thought.

After a long day, Sheila was able to fall fast asleep without being interrupted by anyone.

***

By late Tuesday afternoon, Sheila's anxiety was growing. The more she tried to focus on work, the more the thoughts from her past haunted her. She had to know if Randy was still in jail and she had to know now.

Sheila stepped away from her desk to make another call to Florida. This time she was not going to hang up until she got an answer to the question she asked approximately twenty-four hours ago.

Sheila dialed the number again and repeated the same steps as she did the day before. Of course the DA was not available and neither was his assistant. The secretary took the message along with the request for Sheila's call to be returned today. Disappointed, Sheila headed back to her desk feeling defeated against paranoia versus the threat of evil. While engrossed in thought Sheila inadvertently bumped into Wayne Mackee, one of her employers.

"Oh excuse me sir, I'm sorry." Sheila said apologetically.

"No excuse me. I wasn't paying attention to where I was going. Hi, I'm Wayne." Mr. Mackee said as he extended his hand out to greet Sheila.

Sheila returned the hand shake as she responded, "No I'm sure it was me that bumped into you. Please accept my apology, Mr. Mackee."

"No apologies necessary, Ms...?"

"Oh forgive me. I'm Sheila Mathis, one of the administrative assistants in office suite 1100."

"Oh yes, Ms. Mathis. I've heard a lot about you. Keep up the good work." Mr. Mackee said with a grin.

"Thank you sir, I will." Sheila smiled at the boost of confidence of a good work performance coming from the boss. "Well I better get back to work." Sheila said awkwardly as the two just stood there.

Mr. Mackee nodded in agreement and the two parted. Sheila soon made it back to her desk. As she was putting her cell phone away and the DA's business card back in her purse, her desk phone rang.

"Mackee Taylor & Moss Law Office, this is Ms. Mathis, how may I help you?"

The caller said nothing.

Sheila repeated the same phrase figuring the caller didn't hear her. Still no voice response, only a series of clicking noises. Figuring there was a bad connection, Sheila looked at the caller ID display to return the caller's call from another line. The caller ID registered private number. Sheila once again said hello, this time hearing a dial tone as a response.

Sheila finished out the rest of the day answering calls and entertaining one hang up after another. Refusing to let her paranoia get the best of her, Sheila decided to try to call the DA's office again; taking a chance someone would answer the phone. This time Sheila called from her desk and not from her cell phone hoping to get a response.

After about five rings, a male voice picked up. Sheila asked for Mr. Crain or Mr. Reeder.

The voice on the other end said, "This is Mr. Crain. How may I help you?"

Sheila quickly told Mr. Crain who she was and what she was calling for hoping he would relieve her worry. After a long pause filled with silence, her expectations were far from reach. Mr. Crain informed her that his office found out Randy had been released on bond due to a mix up and a warrant had been issued for his immediate arrest since discovering the mistake.

In between cries of tears, Sheila managed to get out the question of when Randy might be apprehended. Mr. Crain answered, "I don't know but until we get him back in custody, please be careful."

Sheila was frozen, she couldn't respond. Now she had her answer. The unusual incidences were not of paranoia but of pure evil. One she knew would be the death of her and his name was Randy.

"Ms. Mathis. Ms. Mathis? Are you still there?" Sheila heard Mr. Crain say.

"Yes I'm here." Sheila managed to mumble without sobbing.

"Be assured my staff is working diligently to correct this error. I will be in touch as soon as I have more information. Mr. Crain tried sounding reassuring. "And Ms. Mathis?"

"Yes," Sheila managed to get out in between the tears.

"Please try to be careful." Mr. Crain warned.

"Too late, Mr. Crain. Your warning is a little too late." Sheila responded.

Bewildered, Sheila hung up the phone crying silently as she sat staring at the receiver in disbelief.

{ 11 }

Wake Me Up From This Dream

Sheila said nothing on the ride home as she and Mark rode in silence. Initially, Mark attempted to make idle chit chat but soon discovered Sheila was not in any mood to converse about anything. They made it home without getting stuck in traffic which was a relief. Sheila wanted nothing more than to be alone to prepare herself for what else was to come.

Sheila had hoped Mr. Crain's team would take the error serious. However, she doubted recapturing Randy was on their priority list especially since no one bothered to notify her he had been released mistakenly.

The seemingly coincidental incidents meant one thing. Her real nightmare was only beginning and this time, she might not wake up from this dream called reality.

Theresa could tell something was wrong with Sheila the moment she laid eyes on her. Melissa had already been alerted by Mark in a text message that Sheila was not herself and something was wrong. Hearing that, there was an apparent change in Sheila's behavior, Theresa decided to stay home from work to comfort her child.

As Sheila entered the house, she was saddened by the sight of her family. Sheila knew the time had come for her to leave them in order to protect them. Sheila didn't know where she was going or how she would get there but she knew she didn't have a choice. Her pursuit of happier days were over and her hell was here again.

Sheila wasn't up for answering any questions she sensed was on everyone's mind. She purposely avoided eye contact and went straight to her room to lie down saying nothing to no one. No one followed her, not even Theresa sensing Sheila had a lot on her mind.

A few hours passed and Sheila still had not surfaced from her room. Theresa growing worried decided to check on her. Knocking softly, Theresa entered to see Sheila curled up in bed, fully clothed staring at the wall.

The sight of Sheila in such distress bothered Theresa. She didn't know whether she should get her to a hospital or leave her be. Acting on instinct Theresa climbed in bed, and held Sheila. Soon both ladies were crying silent tears.

***

    Sheila awoke to the rays of sunlight that filled her room. She wasn't sure when she drifted off to sleep. She knew it was sometime after Theresa came in her room and held her. It was something about being in her mom's comforting arms that made Sheila feel safe. Something Sheila knew had to come to an end.

    Sheila didn't want to wake up but the persistent urge to use the restroom was hard to ignore and sleep through. Seeing no way of relief but to rise and empty her bladder, Sheila got up quietly hoping not to wake anyone. As soon as Sheila opened her bedroom door, she knew her plan to go unnoticed was not going to work. Just about everyone was already awake, waiting on her to surface.

    Sheila could sense from the look on everyone's face, they knew Randy was out. Making it past the questionable stares, Sheila made it to the restroom. Looking in the mirror at the reflection staring back at her was all too familiar: baggy tired eyes from endless crying as well as visible strains of fatigue.

Sheila knew the stacks were higher now than ever before. Sheila thought about running but didn't know where to go. Sadly, if she did figure out an escape plan, chances were Randy would eventually find her so what was the point.

No. I'm not running. Sheila thought as she washed her face and brushed her hair in an attempt to make an effort to look presentable. She knew upon exiting the bathroom, she would have to address her family; her beautiful family.

Tears started to dwell in Sheila's eyes again. She understood no matter what, she had to separate herself from them in order for no harm to come their way. Sheila also knew there was a chance, a big chance, she may never see them again.

Sheila washed up and opened the bathroom door slowly. Ready or not, she had to face her reality. Her fantasy of having a normal life was over.

{ 12 }

Imprints of the Past

"Sheila, how are you doing?" Melissa was the first to ask, breaking the silence just as everyone settled in the living area.

Sheila didn't answer. She didn't have to. The look of fear and somberness upon her spoke loud enough for all to see.

Nervousness fell upon the room as tranquility signified the fear everyone felt; fear of the unknown.

Finally, Carol spoke filling in the details of the latest events. "There is reason to believe all of the strange occurrences that have occurred lately are not so coincidental after all. Apparently, Randy has been out of jail for quite some time. How long? I'm still trying to get a precise answer."

"What do you mean out of jail? How?" Theresa questioned.

"Something is not right. Surely this is a mistake. I just don't understand…" Melissa added.

Carol continued. "When Randy was initially apprehended by the local authorities for assaulting Sheila, he had outstanding warrants for other crimes in two other states, Utah and Montana. While waiting for a trial date to be determined by the State of Florida Judicial System, an agreement was made for Randy to be transferred to Utah first where he was to be officially charged and booked on kidnapping, rape, sodomy, and assault charges. Then he was to go to Montana to be arraigned on robbery and burglary charges. In the process of executing the agreement, an oversight occurred. The charges pending in Utah were dropped due to a missing witness. When the charges were dropped, Randy was set free by mistake. He never was transferred to Montana and of course Florida assumed Randy was in either Utah's or Montana's custody. They didn't have a clue of the error until Sheila called inquiring on whether he was still in custody due to all the craziness going on around here. Her call prompted an investigation and that's when the discovery was made."

"I…..I still don't understand." Theresa said puzzled. "I look on the inmate website every day and it says he is still in the County Jail."

"In some states, those websites are updated by a third party agency. Therefore the information is not accurate or updated as it should be." Carol explained.

"I don't get it." Theresa expressed in confusion, "If Randy is the culprit for the strange events around here, then how did he get in? We have a high tech alarm system and each time it was on and armed."

Carol paused before responding, glancing at Sheila not wanting to upset her more than she already was. Seeing no change in Sheila's demeanor, Carol continued. "Mom, I don't know how he did it but I believe he did somehow. A friend of a friend got a hold of Randy's rap sheet and even I as a defense attorney will say, Randy has been pretty smart in his criminal actions. He is suspected of taking part in a jewelry heist in which the alarm system was intact when the jewels were stolen. He is wanted in Montana for a bank robbery where the only evidence is the surveillance camera. Somehow he knew the alarm code and vault combinations. He has always managed to stay one step ahead of law enforcement."

Sheila could hear what Carol was saying but her thoughts were racing too fast to participate in the conversation going on. Hearing Randy's accolades made her sick to her stomach. *How could I fall for such an awful guy and never once suspect he was involved in anything other than taking pleasure in beating me senseless?* Sheila asked herself.

Suddenly Sheila made a quick dash to the bathroom as the contents of her stomach decided to make a debut. Hugging the commode, Sheila began to sob uncontrollably. Theresa quickly in tow, kneeled down to hold Sheila in comfort but this time, her mother's arms made her feel worse. Sheila knew this would probably be the last time she would feel her mother's touch while alive. Randy was back and he would make good on his promise – *til* death do them part.

{ 13 }

The Power of Love

"I'm leaving." Sheila announced to everyone in the room.

"Leaving? Oh no you're not!" Theresa interjected.

"Mom, please don't try to stop me. I have to. I have to leave. That's the only way I can keep you safe." Sheila pleaded.

"I said NO!" Theresa yelled as tears filled her eyes.

Sheila shook her head in disagreement. "My mind is made up. It's me he wants so it's me and only me he gets. He tried to hurt you once. I can't let him try again. It's not fair to you, it's not fair to Carol, Melissa, or……"

"Sheila I know all about Randy's threat towards me." Theresa said surprisingly. "If Randy truly wanted to harm me, he would have done so already. What he wants is for you to think he would harm me in order to control you."

"No mom you're wrong. He would harm you. He tried that night with your car by taking the oil out of it. He wanted you to break down on your way to work and……" Sheila started to explain but was unable to finish as the thought of Randy harming her mom became too great for her to digest.

"We know Sheila." Carol stated in reassurance. "We figured it out once you abruptly moved to Florida with him right after that happened and Mr. Greene concluding someone had to have purposely drained the oil out of mom's car. Plus, a woman in love moving to another state with her husband wouldn't have the look of terror you displayed when you told us goodbye. It didn't take much to put the pieces to that puzzle together."

Sheila looked up into Carol's eyes not knowing what to say. Her family knew how deranged Randy was and still no one was upset with her? On the contrary, they wanted her to stay knowing the danger she posed. Sheila was both touched by the display of their love and fearful of their willingness to help her. As tempting as it was to lean on them in her time of despair, Sheila could not allow their love to cloud her judgment. She was leaving and that was final.

Theresa, sensing Sheila's thoughts, spoke and when she did, the whole room fell silent.

"Sheila, listen to me and listen to me good. I lost you once to that monster. I be damned if I lose you again. Please don't leave sweetheart. It's time you stop holding the victim card and start playing by your own set of rules. You are not alone in this battle. I'm right here with you and I'm not leaving and neither are you."

"I'm here too." Carol chimed in.

"Me too." Melissa added.

"Me three," Mark said, as they all embraced in one big group bear hug.

Still Sheila couldn't help but think of the battle that was upon her. Theresa advised her to start playing by her own rules. That was easier said than done. Sheila didn't have a clue of where to begin or how not to hold the victim card. Departing from her family was easy in comparison to never seeing them again. Sheila now knew something she didn't know before, Randy was more dangerous than she ever imagined.

{ 14 }

The Victim Card

After an exhausting day filled with tears and unsettling emotions, Sheila found herself finally alone in her room, reflecting on the advice Theresa gave her.

Her thoughts were soon interrupted by a knock at the door followed by Carol and Melissa entering without waiting for an invitation.

"Can we talk?" Melissa asked, sensing Sheila was deep in thought.

Sheila shrugged her shoulders in response. Knowing it didn't matter what she said, her sisters were going to continue with or without her permission.

Melissa started talking first. "I would be lying if I told you I wasn't worried. From what we already know and Carol has told us is enough for any of us to realize Randy is unstable and poses a threat to us all. I...we want you to know we agree with mom. You must not leave. You have to stop carrying the victim card."

Sheila looked in shock. This was not the time for Melissa's judgments and opinions. "How do I do that Melissa? You know, stop carrying the victim card?" Sheila snapped.

"Don't get smart with me missy. I'm on your side remember? Since you asked how, I will tell you. For starters, you stop running and start fighting for once in your life." Melissa snapped back.

"I'm sorry. Melissa. I know you mean well. I'm just confused, angry, scared, and disgusted. I'm confused on how the legal system allowed this mistake to go unnoticed. I'm angry that not one prosecutor, district attorney, or whatever you call them bothered to follow up with one another until I inquired about my own case. And even then, they didn't return any of my calls; I had to call them again and again to get an answer. I'm scared because I have no idea what Randy plans to do with me, other than kill me. I'm disgusted that I feel so helpless, so very helpless." Sheila declared.

"I can't say I understand how you feel because I don't. What I can say is we are here for you and you do not have to fight this battle alone." Melissa stated with compassion.

"You can't be here Melissa. You and your family must stay away." Sheila said sternly.

"What? That's nonsense." Melissa uttered.

"You want me to stay? You want me to fight. Well, we do so on my terms. I know there is no way I can convince mom to let me leave or separate from me. It's hard enough to even think of what could happen to her but I can't and won't risk jeopardizing any harm coming to you or your family." Sheila stated

"But..." Melissa said trying to interrupt.

"But nothing. You have a husband and two beautiful daughters who need their mom. You can call, you can write, but you will keep your family far away from here until this is over. Promise me that Melissa or so help me, I'm running." Sheila threatened.

"I can't." Melissa answered.

"You can and you will." Carol interrupted. "Sheila's right. The stakes are too high. You have more than yourself to think about."

"Yeah, but don't forget I can handle my own." Melissa retorted.

"This may be true Miss High and Mighty, but psychopaths like Randy don't play by the rules of only harming adults. Remember you have those precious angels to think about and protect." Carol added.

Melissa pondered over what her sisters pointed out. Hating to admit they were right, she reluctantly agreed to keep her distance in order to protect her family.

"Carol, you have to stay away too. Now is a good time for you to move back into your apartment. You know the one you pay rent on but never occupy because you are too busy babysitting me?" Sheila snickered.

"Nice try Goldilocks. I take my babysitting duties serious. I'm not going anywhere. Besides, I moved out of my apartment two months ago." Carol announced. "Furthermore, someone has to help lead the evidence in the right direction when you win this war," Carol said as she winked at Sheila.

Sheila wasn't sure what the wink was for nor did she want to know especially when the wink came from Carol.

"Oh no. All this excitement, I forgot to call job. I'm probably going to be fired for not reporting to work or calling. It doesn't matter, I have to quit anyway." Sheila uttered with sadness.

"There you go, clinging to the victim card." Melissa chimed in. "I called your job this morning and made up some sick story. Don't worry. They are expecting you back on Monday. As far as quitting, why would you do that?"

"Randy jeopardized my job before; you know when I was teaching. I have to expect he will do so again. I would rather give my notice now in hopes I can be rehired if I don't…….." Sheila's words were interrupted by Theresa who had entered the room.

"If you don't what? What you are thinking will not happen. You have to believe that. Randy will not defeat you. You have to believe that too," Theresa stated.

"Mom, you don't know him." Sheila said shaking her head in disagreement of Theresa's views

"I may not know him. But I do know you. You are a fighter, you will win this war." Theresa answered.

"What do I do? With the job I mean." Sheila asked nervously.

"You alert human resources of the situation, carefully of course. You want to tell them just enough information without disclosing all of the details. Don't worry I will help you with this. If at this time they let you go, then so be it." Carol offered.

"I don't know. This all just sounds so risky. Staying here, being at work….." Sheila began to speak but was unable to finish her thought due to the sense of staring glares she noticed as she observed the three women looking at her.

"Ok. OKAY…. I get it. Stop holding the victim card." Sheila couldn't help but smile as the bond of love restricted thoughts of fear from overtaking her mind.

{ 15 }

Taking Chances

Going back at work was met with apprehension. Sheila didn't know what to expect as she sat down with human resources explaining her situation exactly as she had rehearsed with Carol.

To Sheila's surprise, every question Ms. Whyte asked, she had a convincing response to. Thanks to Carol. Carol told her to keep her answers short and sweet; only answering what was asked. *Boy Carol sure knows her stuff,* Sheila thought.

After meeting with human resources, Sheila was given permission to go to work pending an outcome from administration. Sheila wasn't sure if the pending action would result in termination, but if so then so be it as Carol had stated previously. Looking at what she was up against, losing her job was the least of her worries.

Sheila's absence resulted in more work upon her return. She quickly discovered no one filled in for her while she was away. Thankfully, Sheila had a habit of working ahead of schedule therefore it didn't take long before Sheila was back in the swing of things; answering one call after the other all while being called on by two attorneys who both needed assistance simultaneously. By the end of the day, Sheila was ready to go home.

Just as she started gathering her things, she was interrupted by a call from Ms. Whyte prompting her to come to the human resources suite. Sheila felt a rush of dismay come upon her. Sheila had worked there long enough to know calls at the end of the day from human resources meant one thing – termination.

As Sheila gathered up her belongings, she walked slowly towards the elevator dreading of what was to come next. Tears began to fill her eyes at the thought of losing another job she had grown fond of. *Once again Randy wins,* Sheila thought. *Once again.*

Thinking of Randy reminded Sheila that she had not received any strange phone calls during the day nor had she experienced any other strange occurrence.

Before she could try to analyze what this meant, Sheila's thoughts were interrupted by the opening of the elevator door inviting Sheila to enter, which she did. Upon reaching her destination, the doors opened again motioning her to exit.

Sheila walked down the hallway to a set of double glass doors. The head of security for the law firm greeted her in expectation of her arrival. Officer Pete, as he was addressed by the staff, was a tall buff man with a slight accent of some sort. Although he seemed nice, there was something about him Sheila found intimidating. Fighting through the nervousness and increasing anxiety, Sheila managed to mumble "Hello," as he escorted her to the conference room where she found Ms. Whyte, Mr. Mackee, and Kara, Ms. Whyte's assistant, waiting for her.

Sheila entered the room and was prompted to have a seat. Sitting as directed, Sheila could feel her stomach tie up in knots.

Ms. Whyte wasted no time in starting the proceedings of recent developments we feel it is in your best interest and ours if you are moved to safer quarters. With this being said, effective immediately, you will be moved to a more secure location which will result in some minor changes in your duties. In addition, Officer's Pete team is on alert and has a plan in place for any unwelcomed visitors."

Officer Pete nodded in agreement with what was stated.

"What? You mean I'm not fired?" Sheila asked in disbelief.

"Fired? No, you are not. Your work is impeccable. The attorneys you support all seem to have fallen apart the few days you were out last week. Firing you would not be a favorable thing to do. However, please understand had you not brought this up to our attention and something would have occurred, favorable or not, you would have been terminated. Since you notified us of your situation upon discovering your ex was not where you were led to believe he was, which we were able to verify with accuracy, the partners and I agree to keep you on in hopes this problem will be rectified soon as promised by the Florida District Attorney." Ms. Whyte stated.

"Yes, Jim Crain and I are old colleagues and we had a long discussion about your case in detail this morning," interrupted Mr. Mackee. "He gave me his word capturing your ex is a priority for not only his police force but for the Utah and Montana state police departments too. The Colorado state police have already been put on alert and have also joined in on the multi-state man hunt."

Sheila was dumbfounded by what she was hearing. Not only was she not losing her job, she was being offered protection.

"Your sister is Carol Thompson?" Mr. Mackee asked.

Sheila nodded yes.

"She is a smart lady. It is important that you do exactly what she tells you to do if anything should happen. Do you understand?" Mr. Mackee stated in seemingly questionable manner.

Sheila understood exactly what she was told. When in the midst of war with the enemy, honesty is not a virtue to hold onto. Staying alive and out of jail is or at least that's what Carol told her.

{ 16 }

Contemplation

"How did things go today?" Carol asked when Sheila made it home via the arranged car service provided by the law office.

"I'm sure you know exactly how things went." Sheila said sarcastically. "I was advised by one of the partners to do exactly what you tell me to do." Sheila answered. "Any idea why Mr. Mackee would tell me that?"

"I can't imagine why one defense attorney would advise you to listen to another defense attorney. Puzzling isn't it?" Carol said innocently.

Sheila knew there was nothing innocent about what she was told. Working at the law firm, she was able to understand how people can literally get away with murder. Law is truly a game of intelligence and wit. The bigger the stakes, the higher the price tag one will pay to prove their innocence or lack of sufficient evidence whichever comes first.

Sheila never asked Carol about her cases or clients. Keeping in mind what Mr. Mackee said to her, let Sheila know Carol was no amateur. Unsure if this revelation would prove beneficial or not, Sheila was only certain of one thing. Her stakes were high and she had to play to win.

{ 17 }

The Enemy of Fear

Over the next few days, Sheila along with everyone else was on guard in anticipation of Randy's tactics. Not knowing how he would attack or what subtle message of his existence he planned on leaving, left Sheila feeling vulnerable on all levels.

Nightmares started to haunt Sheila again every time she closed her eyes, leaving her feeling restless and tired. Sheila found herself jumping at any unexpected noise and not feeling comfortable in any setting.

Sheila was grateful everyone was determined to help her through this ordeal. The security at work was on high alert and Sheila was escorted just about everywhere. Still with the extra attention, Sheila could not relax knowing Randy was somewhere out there waiting and plotting to get her.

Things were so bad within Sheila that going to the restroom became an ordeal, especially when going to the powder room at work. Sheila routinely checked every empty compartment or waited at the sink pretending to wash her hands if someone was already in one of the stalls, just so she could assure her peace of mind long enough to use the restroom.

By the end of the week and not a peep from Randy, Sheila's thoughts centered on the hope that Randy had been recaptured and was back in police custody. Hope that soon dissipated when Carol announced the police were still in limbo of Randy's whereabouts. Supposedly, his mom and sister didn't have a clue of where he could be either.

Sheila was shocked to hear Randy had living relatives. He never spoke of anyone and once when Sheila inquired of any family, Randy quickly cut the conversation short leading her to believe any family he once had was no longer around.

"Maybe someone did us all a favor and finally laid him to rest, permanently." Carol said as the gang settled in for their weekly meeting.

Everyone was present with the exception of Mark and Melissa who listened in on the speakerphone.

"Carol, that's an awful thing to say." Melissa snickered jokingly.

"Awful or not, it sure would be a relief." Carol replied without regret.

Sheila sat in silence. She didn't know whether to agree or disagree with Carol's comment. Sure Randy being gone would bring relief but no matter how bad Sheila wanted peace, she couldn't and wouldn't wish any bad karma to come to him or anyone for that matter. What Sheila desired most was for Randy to leave her alone.

"Sheila, have you heard from Randy at all?" Theresa asked.

"No. I haven't received any strange calls or hang-ups, no lost keys, no rustling bushes, nothing. I don't know whether to be relieved or more fearful of what's to come." Sheila commented.

Theresa answered shaking her head. "Fear will always set you back. People like Randy feed off fear. That's what turns him on. As long as you harbor a spirit of defeat you won't win."

"Mom I don't even know what I'm fighting for anymore." Sheila said softly.

"You are fighting for life Sheila - YOUR life." Theresa answered with tears in her eyes.

With that remark everyone fell silent, including Carol.

***

As Sheila prepared for bed, she couldn't help but reflect on the words her mom said about her fighting for life. Sheila perceived the message Theresa was conveying but wasn't sure if she could conquer her enemy.

"You are going to make it out of this just fine. You have to believe that." Theresa said startling Sheila.

Deep in thought, Sheila didn't realize Theresa had slipped into bed for the night. The bed they now shared since the discovery of Randy being out on the prowl.

"I hope so." Sheila rebutted.

"I know so." Theresa responded.

"How can you be so sure?" Sheila questioned.

"You wouldn't have made it this far if you didn't have it in you." Theresa replied.

"Mom, I'm so sorry. Sorry for everything. Had I just listened to you and the others…. Had I not gotten involved with Randy, none of this would be happening now." Sheila voiced as she began to cry.

"Sheila, none of us can undo what's been done. We only can learn from what's occurred and keep moving. We all make mistakes in one form or another. Yours just happened to be in the area of romance." Theresa offered in reassurance.

"Mom I doubt very seriously if you have made mistakes like this. You are much smarter."

"Oh dear, you give me way too much credit. I'll admit your dad was no Randy. He was kind, gentle, and loving but he wasn't perfect. He didn't take care of himself like he should have. As a result, he died way before his time. My costly mistakes came in another area – finances. See after your dad died, I came into a lump sum of money that could have set me up for a long time where I didn't have to depend on the wages from work. Instead of putting it in savings, I allowed myself to get sucked in by an investor who ultimately stole most of the money, leaving me strapped for cash." Theresa said reflecting on her own past mistakes.

"Oh mom, I didn't know. You never said anything." Sheila said surprisingly.

"There wasn't anything to say. I could have easily stayed sour about what happened, blaming everyone for my downfall but I chose to get up, brush myself off and start anew. I enrolled at the local college and took finance classes. I have since learned about stocks, bonds, and mutual funds. So much so, that I have secured a little savings that could sustain me from here on out." Theresa said proudly.

"That's great but I don't know where to begin seeing myself out of this situation." Sheila stated.

"You start right where you are now. Don't keep looking back tormenting yourself on the thought pattern of should have or could have done things differently mindset. That's not reality. Pick yourself out of the hole of fear and self-pity you have dug for yourself and start living in the present. You may not know where Randy is or what his next move may be but you do know to expect something cynical to come your way. Prepare yourself for the battle and not for the defeat. When you change your mindset out of the victim mentality you will be surprised how things will start to look differently, even when faced with uncertainty." Theresa offered.

Sheila knew Theresa was right. She just wasn't sure she had any fight left in her.

{ 18 }

Letting Go

Monday morning came sooner than Sheila was ready for. Ironically, she was able to get some rest which is something she hadn't been able to do since the discovery of Randy's presence.

Just like clockwork, she and Carol rode together into town where Carol dropped her off at the office. This morning with both ladies moving in slow motion, the consensus was made to stop at Charlie's, a popular coffeehouse frequented by the local downtown commuters. Once inside, Sheila and Carol both realized they were not the only ones who needed a Monday morning pick me up. The place was crowded and it wasn't even eight o'clock in the city.

Surprisingly with wall to wall patrons, the pair was able to make it out within ten minutes with one of the most delicious tasting expressos in hand.

"This is sooooo good." Sheila squealed.

"It is. I wonder how many calories is in this thing?" Carol asked while giggling.

Both ladies burst into laughter at Carol's question for neither desired to know how sinful their morning rush actually was.

As they approached the entrance to the law firm, Officer Pete greeted them both as he motioned to Carol he would take over Sheila's security detail.

"See you later sis," Carol called out as she continued towards the courthouse.

Once inside, Sheila was swiped in the back elevator entrance and proceeded to the executive suite, her temporary location. Sheila liked the ambiance of the executive suite but missed the interaction she had grown accustomed to on the eleventh floor.

At least on the eleventh floor there was constant traffic from clients, mailroom personnel, lawyers, and other assistants. Now the only people Sheila got a chance to see was security and Mr. Mackee when he came out of his office in passing. Other than that Sheila as pretty much left alone to work; work that seemed to keep building more and more. It was one thing to assist the firm lawyers. It was another to assist the firm lawyers and one of the partners.

By one o'clock, Sheila was famished. As she was securing her computer to go the break area to warm her lunch, the phone rang. Well so much for lunch, Sheila thought.

"Good Afternoon, thank you for calling Mackee, Taylor & Moss, how may I help you?" Sheila greeted the caller as she was trained to do.

"Hello beautiful, I thought I would never get to talk to you. It's like Fort Knox these days with all the security and phone screening going on."

Sheila's heart fell into her stomach...... The voice on the other end of the receiver was familiar, too familiar. The voice was Randy's.

"Beautiful, why aren't you saying anything? I know you are still there because I can hear you breath." Sheila heard Randy ask.

"What do you want Randy?" Sheila heard herself say as she fought hard to hold back the tears.

"Why silly I want you of course. You may be under lock and key but know I am good at breaking and entering. I will get you." Randy taunted.

"Look Randy, I must get back to work. Goodbye." Sheila fired back without hesitation.

"Oh my, listen to you. You're getting rather bold. My how you have changed in this short amount of time we have been separated. Tell me, when did you start drinking coffee with caramel in it? You never liked caramel before." Randy said calmly.

Sheila gasped. She could not believe what she was hearing. Randy was there. He was at Charlie's watching her, yet she did not notice him at all.

"I have to go Randy." Sheila heard herself manage to get out.

"Sheila sweetheart, be careful. We wouldn't want anything to happen to your pretty little face again now would we?" Sheila grew silent with Randy's threat. As he continued, "What security patrol have you confused about my capabilities? Sweetheart, trust me, what I want I get. Oh by the way, tell Carol I said hello and let her know those black shoes did not go well with the green suit she wore today. She should have worn the neutral pair she had on last week."

"Tell her yourself Randy." Sheila snapped.

"You think I won't. You think I'm afraid to tell Carol myself? You must have forgotten who I am and what I will do?" Sheila could hear Randy's rage about to roar.

"I haven't forgotten anything. I'm hanging up now. Goodbye." Sheila said sensing it was time to end the call. Without hesitation, Sheila hung up the phone. Still shaking from the conversation, Sheila somehow managed to alert security of Randy's call. Thankfully, all calls transferred to any of the partner's offices on the business lines are recorded.

For the rest of the afternoon, Sheila was not bothered by anymore calls from Randy. She wasn't sure if it was because he didn't try to call again or security was able to divert any further attempts.

On the ride home, Sheila couldn't help but reflect on the conversation with Randy. He let his intent be known, he was coming after her. This was no surprise to Sheila.

What was surprising was her reaction. Initially after the dialogue, Sheila was visibly upset but not for long. She managed to calm her insides down and continue working, getting a lot done. Perhaps the fight Theresa kept insisting Sheila had in her really did exist, perhaps.

The driver interrupted Sheila's thoughts as he announced she had made it to her destination.

Opening the door, she was escorted out of the car. Sheila knew this was no ordinary driver because she could see the bulge on his side where his revolver sat. Carol had explained the partners' drivers had to be armed because the partners are always targets, especially if they lose a high profile case.

Sheila quickly made it to her front door; then signaled to the driver he could leave as she entered her home where she was greeted by her family.

"I can't believe that bastard had the nerve to talk about my shoes." Carol exclaimed.

"I can. That was his way of letting me know he is watching not only me but all of us." Sheila responded.

"I'm just happy you didn't break down and let him get the best of you." Theresa stated.

"I almost did. It wasn't easy." Sheila stated not wanting to give the illusion she was confident in her actions when it came to Randy.

"Were you surprised by the call?" Carol asked.

"No, not really. Just taken off guard. I guess going a whole week with no sign of him or his foolishness and then out of nowhere he calls, just kind of took me by surprise, that's all." Sheila confessed.

"I wonder how did he get pass the switchboard to the executive suite?" Theresa questioned.

"After an investigation, it was discovered that the call was transferred by a temp from the agency. Apparently, she became overwhelmed by the constant ringing in inadvertently transferred the call without following the screening techniques. She was let go as a result. I feel bad. Now that poor girl is out of a job all because of me." Sheila said sadly.

"No, that poor girl is out of a job because she didn't follow protocol. I know it is hard for you to understand but trust me, protecting the partners is number one." Carol stated.

"Well I'm not a partner." Sheila replied.

"No you're not but you are a secretary to one of the most notorious lawyers in this city and the threatening call was transferred to his line. A call like that could have very well been for him. That's how security views it. Like it or not, Mr. Mackee has taken a liking to you for some reason. If he hadn't, you would not be sitting where you are sitting right now in that firm. If he says you are to be protected, he means it." Carol explained.

"I see." Sheila said.

"Mr. Mackee likes you?" Theresa said amusingly.

"Mom, not like that! Our relationship is strictly professional." Sheila said in disbelief by Theresa's teasing tone.

"A mom can wish can't she?" Theresa hinted.

"You can wish all you want but I doubt if Mr. Mackee or any other man for that matter, would look twice at me in an attractive way."

"Why do you say that?" Theresa asked.

"I'm a broken woman mom, you know damaged, hurt, destroyed, messed up… do I need to go on?"

"You may be broken as you put it, but you are in no way shattered." Theresa pointed out.

"What's the difference?" Sheila asked innocently.

"Broken represents a temporary state of despair that has the ability to be repaired. Shattered is permanent, the repair is irreparable." Theresa stated.

"I still don't get it." Sheila said confused.

"Let me illustrate, if I drop this priceless glass and it breaks, there is a chance, a great one that I can glue the pieces together therefore keeping most of its original value. On the other hand, if I drop this same glass and it shatters into a thousand pieces, the damage will be too great to repair and the glass is forever destroyed." Theresa explained.

"Oh I see." Sheila responded.

"Do you really?" Theresa asked.

"I get it. I really do." Sheila said wondering in thought.

"But?" Carol asked.

"But don't you think before I attempt to open any new doors, I need to close the door on the old one and for good?" Sheila asked.

"Here, here," Carol said as she raised her glass of wine in the air as a gesture to toast to Sheila's profound statement.

"Here, Here!" The trio said in unison as they tapped each other's glass in agreement.

{ 19 }

Courage Under Fire

Sheila tossed and turned all night. One dream after another was of Randy waking her, following her, or attacking her. Finally, after seemingly restless hours, Sheila decided she would go to the kitchen to fix her a cup of tea.

"Can't sleep either I see." Theresa's asked startling Sheila.

"All I seem to do is dream and not of anything good. Did I wake you?" Sheila asked.

"No you didn't. My body is still on nightshift time. I usually wake up sometime after midnight and may be able to go back to sleep around five in the morning or so." Theresa responded.

Sheila suddenly felt tears begin to roll down her cheeks.

"Sheila, what's wrong?" Theresa questioned, unsure why Sheila started to cry.

"Mom, everything. If it weren't for me you would not have retired and would still be going to a job you loved. Because of me everything has changed." Sheila sobbed.

"I have no regrets for retiring believe me! I should have retired a long time ago. This situation wasn't the sole reason I decided to submit my paperwork. The company is changing benefits and retirement packages – a tactic used by many corporations to force old timers like myself out. If I had stayed, I would have lost part of my pension along with my sick time and vacation time buy out. Retiring was a good decision for me. I'm enjoying being home with my girls and having the energy to keep up with those busy grandkids of mine." Theresa reassured Sheila.

"I just feel like….like I've caused a mess of more than my life." Sheila responded with confusion.

"Sheila, what did I tell you about holding the victim card?"

"I've been holding it for so long I don't know how to let it go." Sheila whispered to her mom.

"You will figure it out my darling."

"Mom, what if I don't?"

"The only reason you won't is because you didn't try to." Theresa responded.

"How can you be so sure?" Sheila questioned.

"Like I said before, you would have never made it this far if you didn't have the fight in you."

Sheila pondered over Theresa's last statement still unsure why Theresa kept emphasizing she had fight in her. Hadn't she proved otherwise? Particularly back in Florida at the hospital when they were reunited where Theresa saw firsthand how weak Sheila was when it came to Randy's rage. Or the need for increased security with cameras, motion sensors, and deadbolt locks all because of Sheila's inability to separate herself from a dangerous man. A man she once loved and brought around her family insisting he was the "One."

Sheila was very unsure she had enough fight in her to win against Randy. In fact, she knew she didn't. Take away all the protection patrol at work as well as home and she would be dead without a doubt. A condition Sheila wasn't convinced wasn't inevitable; her inevitable fate.

    Theresa left Sheila alone with her thoughts as she sat in silence drinking her tea. Sheila had a lot on her mind. Mostly concerns without any seemingly viable solutions. Sheila couldn't help but recollect on Theresa's words consistently reminding her that she had enough fight in her to beat Randy. Was Theresa just saying things to make Sheila feel better or did she know something that Sheila didn't?

{ 20 }

Reality Scares Me

Sheila could hear the alarm clock buzzing from her room as she sat in silence at the kitchen table. The alarm clock was her cue, her signal, it was time to get up and get ready for a day filled with unknown challenges.

Sheila didn't know what to expect from Randy. All she knew was to expect something because Randy was true to his word, he gets what he wants and he wanted Sheila.

By six thirty, Carol emerged from her room with a cell phone stuck to her ear, reciting orders to her assistant. This was her daily ritual. Sheila admired Carol. Carol possessed everything: strength, power, and courage. Qualities Sheila wished she had. Carol didn't seem to blink twice or get upset when Sheila told her what Randy said about her. Yes, Sheila wished she could be more like Carol. Maybe then, Randy would leave her alone.

"Sheila, are you ready? We can't be late. I have to be in court at eight sharp." Carol said hurriedly.

"Yes, I just need to grab my purse." Sheila responded.

"Mom we're gone. Carol yelled. "Put the alarm on instant."

"Ok. Doing it now," Theresa yelled back.

On the ride into work, Carol seemed bubblier than ever. She hummed and danced to the music. Curious as to what brought about the morning mood change, Sheila asked. "What has gotten into you? Why all the cheer?"

"All the cheer? What's wrong with a little jovial spirit in the morning?" Carol asked.

"Nothing's wrong. It's just not you. Usually you are a grouch until you get some coffee in you. Did you already have a cup or two?" Sheila inquired.

"No I haven't had any yet. Trust me, we are making our Charlie's run." Carol answered smiling.

Sheila got quiet. She wasn't expecting to go to Charlie's this morning or any other morning since Randy pointed out he saw her there.

"Sheila, what's going in that mind of yours?" Carol asked.

"I, I… I just thought we would steer clear of Charlie's. You know since Randy……"

"No ma'am we are not! Randy nor anyone else will control or stop us from doing what we enjoy." Carol snapped.

"Carol?"

"Yes Sheila….?"

"Can you teach me to be more like you?" Sheila asked in a serious tone.

Puzzled by this question, Carol asked, "What do you mean?"

"You know, teach me to not be afraid." Sheila answered.

"I'm thrilled you think so notably of me." Carol said snickering. "The truth is my life experiences have taught me not to show any signs of fear particularly when faced with opposition. Don't forget I am a defense attorney. A damn good one might I add. And with the reputation of being good at the game of wits, my clients are not exactly the ones who are listed in the role model category. A lot of times, I am scared out of my mind to lose a case because I never know the reaction of such model citizens. But I have learned people feed off fear and if you show your emotions or any signs of weakness, the opposition will win."

"Oh so the hard ass exterior is just protecting your soft side?" Sheila joked.

"I wouldn't take it that far. But contrary to popular belief I do have feelings that involve caring and love." Carol said.

"Oh so you do know how to love?" Sheila said jokingly.

"Of course I do silly, I love you don't I?" Carol said accepting the joke.

"Ahhh I'm flattered, you love me." Sheila said delighted.

"Hah. Hah. Don't push your luck. I have a reputation to protect, as well as a family. And I will do anything necessary to see to it my family is kept safe. So you may want to rethink wanting to be like me." Carol answered no longer joking.

"Carol I don't want to ask what you mean by that last comment, do I?" Sheila asked.

"If you're not ready for the answer, you don't." Carol answered.

Sheila thought for a moment before proceeding nervously, "Carol, do you have a gun?"

"Who me? Little innocent me? Of course I don't have A gun silly. I have several." Carol responded in laughter.

Sheila wasn't sure if Carol was joking or not. Something told her to let the conversation go and change the subject. Carol had a reputation around the law firm of dealing with some shady clients. Clients Sheila's law firm refused to represent.

Changing the subject, Sheila asked again, "Why are you in such a good mood?"

"I'm always in a good mood." Carol responded.

"Hardly." Sheila mumbled.

"Since you must know, the case I have been working on has been kicking my butt. I couldn't see any way to win or come out with a favorable plea bargain for my client. But as luck has it, the prosecution's key witness didn't show up for trial on yesterday and is now refusing to testify against my client. No testimony – no conviction. So this morning, I get to go into the courtroom asking the judge to dismiss the charges." Carol said as she tapped the steering wheel to the beat of the song playing on the radio.

"What if the judge refuses?" Sheila questioned.

"Then at best the trial will be postponed until further notice. Either way it buys my team time to reconstruct a winning strategy, a plan B, since Plan A failed." Carol said.

"Carol don't you feel bad sometimes?"

"Feel bad about what?"

"For representing such awful people?"

"No I don't. Trust me Sheila, there are bad people on both sides of the spectrum. Not everyone on the badge side is on the up and up."

"But still it seems so immoral."

"What seems immoral?" Carol questioned.

"Representing murderers, liars, thieves, and drug dealers." Sheila mumbled not wanting to come off as being judgmental.

"Hmmm I see. So tell me how do you feel when the drug dealers are busted with multiple bags of product yet only a fourth gets listed into evidence? What happens to the other three-fourths? Have you ever asked yourself what happens to all the money that is confiscated in the bust? Or how do the drugs seem to continue to make it into this country seemingly unnoticed?" Carol said opening a door of inquiry in Sheila's mind.

"I have to believe there are good people in the world Carol. I just have to."

"There are. But trust me, there are more Randy's than there are Sheila's."

"I don't know Carol."

"Sheila the difference between you and me is we see the world from different views. I'll prove it to you. You keep hoping and wanting the good side of Randy to come out. That's why you can't see any harm coming to him even in the midst of him trying to harm you. I, on the other hand, see that he is rotten to the core and there is no good side." Carol pointed out.

"You're right. I do want him to go away and leave me alone." Sheila agreed.

"He won't do that on his own, you will have to help him leave you alone." Carol stated.

"How?" Sheila questioned.

"As mom says, quit holding onto the victim card."

Sheila once again pondered over these words.

{ 21 }

Help Wanted

Charlie's was crowded as expected. Sheila tried acting normal and pretending she wasn't apprehensive about her surroundings, but the feelings of uneasiness were eating her up internally.

She ordered a caramel latte only this time with extra caramel. If Randy was watching, he could watch her order what she wanted, how she wanted it. Randy mentioned in his conversation with her how she didn't like caramel. That was far from the truth. She loved caramel. She just was never allowed to have it when she was with him because it was fattening and he didn't want her "packing on the weight."

Sheila was so engrossed into the latte she hadn't noticed she and Carol had made it to the office entrance or that Carol was in conversation with a big stocky looking guy she had never seen before.

"See you later sis," Carol called out as the exchange was made.

Sheila waved as she followed Ken, the security guard on duty this morning, into the building and down the hallway to the back entrance elevators.

"Have a good morning Ms." Ken said as he let her onto the private elevator and used his key to unlock the floor to the executive suite.

"You too Ken." Sheila replied.

***

As Sheila settled into her desk to begin her morning ritual she was interrupted by numerous requests from one attorney, named Jim Malone who was fairly new to the firm. Mr. Malone expressed in ten voice messages and five emails he needed her help ASAP. Sheila, sympathizing with his urgency decided to call him right away before he blew a gasket.

"Hi Mr. Malone. This is Sheila Mathis. You requested I call you as soon as I arrived."

"Yes, Oh thank God Sheila. Listen, Mr. Mackee called me early this morning and requested I join the team working on the McNelley case. He didn't give me any details so I'm not sure where to go or where to report. One of the assistants told me you would have the information. Can you give it to me?"

Sheila hesitated for a moment. She wasn't sure if she was in fact speaking with Jim Malone or not and needed to verify the information he was giving her.

That was what she had been informed to always do before giving out any information to anyone.

"Mr. Malone, I would be glad to assist you. I tell you what let me find the information and I will email you with the details." Sheila offered.

"Oh okay. I don't mind holding if that would be better." He stated.

"No I prefer to email you the exact details to ensure you get everything you need to make a good impression on the boss." Sheila replied.

"Good thinking. I'll wait for your email." He replied.

Sheila quickly picked up the phone and pushed the private line button that rang directly to Mr. Mackee. Sheila herself had no idea what the actual number was for it was programmed on the speed dial on her desk phone. After three rings the call went to voice mail. Sheila left Mr. Mackee a message in code saying she needed to verify information before she could release it. Within minutes, Mr. Mackee returned her call and verified the accuracy of Jim Malone's call authorizing

Sheila to email the details of the team's meeting and what Mr. Malone needed to prepare for.

Sheila signed onto her inbox and noticed she had fifty six unread messages to start her day. This is going to be a busy morning Sheila thought recognizing most of the emails were from other attorneys she still assisted from when she was on the eleventh floor.

After sending the information to Jim Malone, Sheila started going through her inbox messages. Most were simple request, some not so simple. By the twentieth email, Sheila noticed the sender's address was from her personal email. Thinking it was junk email, she opened it. To her surprise the sender was none other than her nuisance admirer Randy.

Hello Beautiful.

Why are you having trouble sleeping? The bags under your eyes are not attractive and I'm concerned about you. Don't worry sweetheart, we will be back together soon – real soon and I will take care of you like old times. Until then try to stay safe.

Love always,
Til Death Do Us Part

Sheila immediately hit print to have a copy of the email to show the others as she tried to calm her nerves. There was no stopping this guy. He follows her, watches her, harasses her, and threatens her. Sheila didn't understand how one man can evade law enforcement for as long as he has been able to. Maybe Carol was right. Maybe everyone on the badge side was not on the right side of the law.

Sheila didn't hesitate to grab her cell phone to call the Florida DA's office in attempt to get an update or reassurance of efforts being made to capture Randy. As usual, she was unable to do anything but leave a message. A message she was sure would not be returned.

Sheila then decided to phone Carol. If she was to stop playing the victim she needed guidance from someone who could help her.

"Sheila, is everything okay?" Carol asked as she answered the call.

"Everything's fine. I need your help." Sheila managed to say.

"Sure what's going on?" Carol questioned.

"I got an email from Randy." Sheila explained.

"What did it say?" Carol's tone went from concern to coldness in mere seconds.

"I'll send it to you." Sheila told Carol.

"Ok I have my computer open."

"No I'll fax it. I don't want to forward it just in case he has some kind of virus embedded in it. I'm going to alert the computer technology department on my end to check my system just in case." Sheila responded.

"Ok fax it to my office, I'm headed there now. Sheila you said you needed my help, what do you need from me?" Carol continued to question the nature of Sheila's call.

"Teach me how to shoot one of those guns you have." Sheila pleaded.

Carol started laughing. "Sheila I won't do that. One of us has to remain innocent if anything ever goes down."

"I'm serious Carol."

"Sheila so am I. Send me the fax and continue about your day. Soon this will all be over." Carol said without any hesitancy.

"How can you be so sure?" Sheila asked, still unsure of how Carol could be so confident.

"Is this the victim Sheila asking or the victor?" Carol questioned.

Sheila thought for a moment.

"I get it. The victor knows this will end, the victim isn't sure it ever will." Sheila answered prideful finally understanding the message Theresa kept telling her.

"Exactly!" Carol yelled in excitement.

"Fax is coming over now. Carol?"

"Yes?"

"Thank –you."

"Thank me for what?"

"For helping me see the light."

"Don't thank me. Thank mom. She brought it out of you. Not me." Carol remarked.

"No argument there."

As the pair hung up, Sheila couldn't help but smile. She got it. She finally understood what her mom and Carol had been trying to get her to understand all along.

{ 22 }

Fight or Flight

For the remainder of the day, Sheila didn't have time to reflect on Randy's shenanigans even if she wanted to. Her day was busy keeping up with the attorneys' demands as they were coming in faster than she could catch her breath.

By six o'clock, it was time to call it quits. Sheila could not go on anymore and it seemed like no one else could either for finally her phone stopped ringing and the emails stopped flooding in. Sheila was exhausted. All she wanted to do was get home, eat, and try to relax. She knew that she would not have problems going to sleep tonight because she was tired.

Sheila called for the driver who was already waiting on her downstairs. She quickly made her way to the car and rested her head against the seat. As she settled into the car, Sheila suddenly felt a pain in the pit of her stomach. Dismissing this feeling as hunger pains,

Sheila made a note to self to eat as soon as she got home.

Sheila must have dozed off because the next thing she knew, she was in front of her house as the driver motioned for her to exit. Without missing a beat, Sheila jumped up out of the seat and walked briskly up the driveway to the front door. As she approached the entry way the pain hit her again only this time with much more force. Sheila made it to the front door expecting the usual greeting from her family. Instead she was greeted by none other than RANDY!

Sheila immediately thought to retreat towards the driver but Randy was one step ahead of her.

"Hello beautiful. Now be a good girl and wave to the driver everything is ok."

Sheila hesitated.

"Darling," she could hear Randy call her, "Do as I say and I will leave your mom out of this." Randy's threat pierced her skin like a nail.

Sheila instantly did as she was told. Although she couldn't see Teresa, she knew if Randy had gained entry into the house, Theresa was not safe and she better do as she was told. As she waved the armed driver away, Sheila knew she was in trouble. Randy had returned to finish the job he started back in Florida. Only this time, Sheila knew things would be worse.

"Come in dear, close the door. We have a lot to catch up on." Randy said tormenting her.

"Where's my mom?" Sheila managed to get out through the tears.

"Oh she is resting. Wanna see?"

Sheila nodded her head yes.

Randy then grabbed Sheila by her hair pulling her towards the patio door.

Sheila gasped.

There lied Theresa on the floor unconscious with a blood seeping from her head.

"You. You MONSTER!" Sheila shouted in rage.

KAPOW! Randy hit Sheila with what felt like maximum intensity that her whole body thrust against the patio glass as she landed on top of Theresa. Sheila could feel Theresa's breathing as her body laid listless.

"Sweetheart is that any way to talk to your dear husband? What has gotten into you?" Randy said as he grabbed her by her hair again, yanking her to her feet.

"You're sick Randy. You need help." Sheila managed to say as the taste of blood filled her mouth.

BAM! Another hit came, followed by a Randy's hands gripping her neck in a chokehold position.

Sheila knew she couldn't win against Randy but she had to fight at least to save Theresa if not herself. "Ok. Ok Randy. What do you want?"

"What do I want? What kind of foolish question is that? I told you, you weren't going anywhere, didn't I?" Randy stated.

Sheila didn't respond. She couldn't.

"Answer me dammit!" Randy yelled, making Sheila jump. "Didn't I tell you we would be together forever?"

"Yes." Sheila whispered.

"Then tell me why you let them lock me up like a caged animal. Why did you turn against me? Why did you tell them I did all those things to you?" Randy hissed.

"Because you did." Sheila mumbled.

Randy then grabbed Sheila by her shirt, lifting her off the floor and pulled her into the bedroom.

Sheila started kicking and yelling "No, Randy please don't."

"Please? You don't have to beg baby. I've been waiting a long time to feel my wife again. I want it as much as you do."

"No, no Randy. Please No!" Sheila continued to beg.

Randy then lifted her higher in the air, dropping her on the bed. As he proceeded to pull his pants down, Sheila made a mad dash towards the front door.

Feeling Randy in close proximity as she fumbled to get the door open, she managed to push the help button on the alarm key pad then proceeded to run towards the kitchen to the back door.

Randy was too fast for her. As he caught up with her, he slapped her against the kitchen island knocking silverware and plates onto the floor along with her. Randy then pinned her down with one knee embedded in the pit of her stomach. The same area where she experienced the sharp intense pain minutes earlier.

Just as Randy reached into his back pocket pulling out a gun, the phone started ringing. Sheila hoped it was the alarm company. Better yet she was hoping Randy hadn't seen her when she pushed the help button.

"Who would be calling now? Randy inquired. "Maybe it is Carol or Melissa? Oh how I would love for the two of them to join this party." Randy mocked. "Now I was hoping I wouldn't need to use this," Randy continued his taunts while pointing the gun to Sheila's head. "Stop fighting me. You know you want me just as much as I want you."

"No I don't Randy. I don't want you. I want you to leave me alone." Sheila pleaded in response.

Sheila wasn't expecting what came next. Randy thrust himself into her with such force that pain waves spread throughout her entire body. All Sheila could think of is fight. Mom and Carol said to fight.

Randy's weight was too much for Sheila to get off of her. So she knew she had to think of another way out. The silverware. Sheila could see a paring knife near her right heel. Sheila scooted and squirmed to try and get the knife within arm's reach.

"Oh yes baby that's it, move with me." She heard Randy moan as he continued to violate her.

Finally the scooting paid off, Sheila grabbed the knife and stabbed Randy in the neck as hard as she could.

For a moment Randy stopped moving and stared at her as if he were about to keel over, then out of nowhere Randy hit her across her head with the barrel of the gun as he continued to make his way into her. Sheila falling in and out of consciousness knew she was losing and losing big. When Randy finally got off of her, Sheila thought he would then leave for he gotten the best of her.

No such luck. Randy then went into hysterics, kicking her, punching her, and slapping her with all his might. The more she tried to fight back as Carol and mom coached her to do, the more he beat her. Sheila felt her destiny was death especially when she came too again. Randy demanded she look at him as he stood over her with the barrel of the gun pointed directly at her.

"How dare you try to kill me!" He yelled. "It's you who will die for betraying me."

Just as Sheila braced herself for the inevitable, she heard a click and a loud boom as an accented male's voice shouted, "I told you not to hit women!"

Just then Randy hit the ground lying only a few feet away from Sheila, with a nice size hole in his head and smirk on his face.

Sheila tried to make out the figure of the mystery person who came to save her but was unable to see clearly through the shade of blood drenching her face. What she could make out appeared to be more of a female's shape, one that resembled Carol's physique perfectly. Yet the voice was that of a man's.

Sheila tried to lift herself off the floor but couldn't. The more she tried, the harder it was to breath. Sheila knew she couldn't hold on. Before long, Sheila was left with no other choice but to let go and allow destiny to take its course.

{ 23 }

Courage is the Most Important of All Virtues

- Maya Angelou

"You won! I knew you would." Theresa whispered in Sheila's ear while wearing a big wide grin.

"What? Where am I? Am I in heaven?" Sheila asked puzzled by her surroundings.

"Heaven? Why no! You are in the hospital silly." Teresa answered. "Did you hear me? You won!"

Won? Won what? Sheila thought as she tried to focus on what was going on.

"Where's Randy? Where's Carol?" Sheila moaned attempting to get up setting off several machine alarms which sent the nurse flying in the room to see what was going on.

Seeing Sheila was conscious, the nurse greeted her and told her to take it easy as she exited the room.

"Mom, where's Randy?" Sheila asked not sure what was real and what was a dream.

"Randy is gone. He's dead." Theresa answered.

"How?"

"Well that's what we were hoping you can tell us. Randy knocked me out as I was putting the trash outside. When I came to, I was in the back of the ambulance with Carol by my side. Carol told me she got a call from the alarm company saying an alert had been made from the house but when they called no one answered. She arrived with the police and found you on the floor covered in blood with Randy lying beside you dead with a knife sticking out of the side of his neck and a gunshot wound to his head. Before you passed out you managed to tell her a strange man shot Randy."

Hearing this, Sheila knew the occurrence was real. She closed her eyes, trying to remember the last moments before Randy was killed. Sheila could recall hearing an unfamiliar male's voice with an accent before the loud boom sound that must have been the gunshot that saved her. Yet even with determined recollection Sheila couldn't make out any distinguishing details other than thinking the figure of the unknown hero resembled Carol's. *Carol? No, it couldn't have been Carol. The voice was clearly that of a male's. Sheila reflected. Did I really manage to tell Carol a strange man shot Randy? Why can't I remember that?* Sheila thought becoming more confused than ever.

"Hello Sheila."

Sheila's thoughts were interrupted by a familiar voice, Mr. Mackee.

"Hi." Sheila responded shyly.

"You've been through a lot. You had us worried. Your mom said you would pull through. She said you were a fighter." Mr. Mackee continued.

"She sure is." Carol exclaimed grinning from ear to ear as she walked in full of glee. "Sheila there is a detective here waiting to talk to you about what happened. I filled him in on what you told me about the man who shot Randy. The police want to know if you can provide more details." Carol winked as she finished her speech.

"I'm going to go to the cafeteria to find a cup of coffee. Ms. Thompson, would you care to join me?" Mr. Mackee asked Theresa, who graciously accepted the offer.

"We'll give you some privacy while you talk to the detectives. There is no need for two attorneys to be present. I'm sure Carol can handle things from here." Mr. Mackee stated. Mr. Mackee then bent over as to appear to kiss Sheila on the cheek only to whisper, "It's good to have you back. Remember, follow Carol's lead and do exactly as she tells you."

Sheila understood and did what was instructed of her especially when Detective Moore came into the room asking her to recount what happened that dreadful night. Sheila told him everything from the time she entered the house, to being beaten and raped, stabbing Randy with the knife, and of course when the strange man appeared out of nowhere shot Randy. Detective Moore questioned whether she could give a description of what the stranger wore, how tall he was, his hair color, or nationality.

Sheila explained she couldn't give a description, she only remembered him saying something about "not hit" and the word "women." The only thing that she could tell him was the man's voice was heavy with some sort of accent she wasn't familiar with.

The detective thanked her and told her he may have to come back to ask more questions. Sheila nodded her head in acknowledgment.

After Detective Moore left, Carol squealed, "You won. Victory is yours!"

"I may have won the war but it was one hell of a battle." Sheila sighed.

"It was darling, but you still won." Carol said in cheer.

Carol and Sheila sat in silence both knowing the horror was truly over and what really happened that night was to never be spoken of ever.

Afterword

Writing this story was very hard to do especially since the fear, abuse, and embarrassment Sheila endured is all too familiar. Countless women are mistreated everyday by their "One." Women like my sister Nikki. Although Sheila's story and Nikki's story differ, they both have something in common. They both were broken women.

Nikki, like so many women, lived in secret and shame for many years barely surviving. Years after her ordeal, Nikki opened up to me about some of the things that happened to her.

Listening to her, I couldn't help but wonder how she went through years of abuse and we, I, had no idea. No, correction, I had an idea but not to the magnitude she suffered. Her Randy aka "Kenneth" made sure he kept her away from her family, those that loved her. He wanted complete control and he had it.

I encouraged her to write her story to share with others. You never know someone reading her true story may need an ounce of hope in seeing how one can sustain years of abuse and make it out better than ever. Months later, this is what she sent me expressing the mission was harder than she imagined.

This is what she shared. This is Nikki's story:

Bound by Chains
Written by Nikki C.

Copyright ©2013 Nikki C., All Rights Reserved

BOUND BY CHAINS
THE BEGINNING…

It has taken me six and a half years to get to this point in my life. To write the final chapter of my misery. This is something I always wanted to, but felt as though I would be attacked just for even thinking about voicing my fears, concerns, terror, and struggles to release the shackles that have been holding me back from life. What misery you might ask? The one I call the "Green Eyed Devil."

Now this particular "Green Eyed Devil" I am referring to is my ex. I will refer to him as Kenneth for the duration of this story. Now don't get me wrong, Kenneth was the type of guy any girl would fall for. He was charming, cute, and had just enough of roughness to him. Needless to say, I met him at a club in the late 90's and felt an instant attraction to him. We hit it off immediately and I ended up pregnant way before we had a chance to get to know one another.

Judge me if you want, but I can point out a few people who have been in my shoes or trying them on. Oh, Kenneth had the right words, the right moves, and I took his possessiveness to be cute.

We would go out to eat, to the park, or just spend time walking or riding around.

Sounds nice, huh?

Yes it was nice as long as I did not let my eyes wonder away (both sex included). I knew it was getting to a changing point when we were riding in the car together and we stopped at a stop light. Now naturally when we (people) stop at a stop light, we glance at the car next to us. It is just a natural habit to look at your surroundings. Oh how I remember how he went off on me and accused me of wanting to sleep with the person in the next car. Pregnant and all! Do you know how hard it is not to glance at a stop light? I believe my neck hurt more from trying to resist the natural turn of the head versus the pokes at my head or grabbing of my arm.

 I stayed, the drama continued, and the violence slowly increased. If you keep on forgiving a person for their wrongdoings and they know that you will accept any kind of treatment, they will continue to increase those wrongdoings just to see if you will accept it.

 Around mid- pregnancy, I found out that a girl I use to be around was pregnant for him also. Of course, I still stayed and told him to take care of ALL of his responsibilities. I experienced so much drama from that incident, but did not find out until 2011 that it was because he was lying about our relationship. Therefore, to her, I was breaking up her newfound family.

 During my pregnancy, I experienced many harsh words from him with a few pushes, shoves, grabbing, and poking. I thought it was nothing serious and maybe I was just not doing something right. Maybe I was not saying the right words, wearing the right clothes, styling my hair the way he wanted, pleasing him correctly, or cooking properly. Little did I know that every day he was mentally breaking me down and getting me to a spot where I would lose my identity completely.

    I should have stopped being naïve when I realized he was never going to take me to meet his family. Oh, I did sit outside in the car while he went in quickly (30 min or more). Laugh if you want. I do NOW. He had me terrified to move, blow the horn, or anything. I did meet his mother accidentally one day when there was a mix up with his oldest child being dropped off. To my surprise, she did not even know me or that I was pregnant (in my sarcastic voice).

Joy Cometh and it Goes

When I went into labor, I was ecstatic. Here was a baby about to come into this world that we would both love, confess our undying love to one another, get a house, get married, and live like one happy family. Well that was fun in my head to imagine until I realized that he decided not to leave work to be with me.

My friend had just delivered her baby two weeks before me (I swear this was not planned) and she was by my side the whole time. My mother left her job to pick me to take me to the hospital close to noon. My friend asked if she would stop and get her since she literally had to pass in front of her to get to me. Oh, he did call into the room after my friend left a message for him.

It gets better. After my baby girl came into the world, I was so happy and I poured so much love into that tiny life that was looking at me with unconditional love. Then he decides to grace us with his presence that night. He came in with a look that said he had better things to do, so naturally, he picked a fight. He took one look at our girl and said she was not his and he cursed me so loudly. I was called everything in the book and he refused to sign any paper work. The next afternoon he apologized, fed me some lines, and I took the bait, After all, I did want that picture I drew in my head of the perfect family.

When I went back for my check up, I found out I was pregnant again. Yes again, and that soon. I felt I had to give him what he wanted before I would be accused of sleeping with someone else even though he knew where I was before I even knew where I was going.

Can you imagine being pregnant while trying to nurture an infant/newborn?

I was a single parent and did not realize it. Although he said he accepted our child, he tried his best not to touch her unless it was for a picture or to appease me. He did not want anything to do with her. At first, it was because she was too little. Then because he was busy or tired. The same affection I was begging for my baby to receive, he gave it all to my stepchild. A stepchild, I loved and resented at the same time. I did not know I could feel that way about a child. That soon passed because I realized I spent more time with her than he did, so we loved each other unconditionally.

A few months later, I gave birth to a baby boy and Kenneth was there for the birth. He was more excited than I was (and I did not think that was possible). That was his baby boy he always wanted. I just knew things would be different now. Since baby boy was premature, he stayed at the hospital while Kenneth and I returned home. Excuse me. My mother's house.

Kenneth rocked me when I cried and took me to see baby boy to comfort me. Yes, things were going to be great. That, however, turned out to be one of the shortest fantasies I could have dreamed up. So now, I have two children who are nine months apart. The same baby boy Kenneth was so excited about is the same one he refused to hold. Since our son was extra small, and preemie diapers were too big, he expressed that he was too little to hold.

As baby boy became bigger, Kenneth felt he still was not big enough. Then it was he cries too much, he does not want me, I am tired, to my favorite, and by far…he's boring. Kenneth was always in the streets but since baby boy always fell asleep in the car, he was not allowed to ride until he became fun and stayed awake. Baby boy never became fun to him.

Now my big girl spent her time loving her baby brother. He was her baby and they were inseparable. However, every little girl loves to have her father's attention and love. If only you could see her pleading eyes for the same hugs and kisses her big sister received it would break your heart. I cried and fought for her plenty of days. After he would hug, kiss, and play with his oldest child, my big girl would run up and say, "Do me daddy! Do me!" with excitement in her voice and would always walk away with the saddest look. Everyone fell in love with this child. She was always happy, never cried unless she was wet or hungry, and was always ready to love you. If there were ever a thing as a perfect baby, she would definitely be it!

MAKING PAIN OFFICIAL

My children were deprived of proper love, so was I, but for some reason Kenneth had a hold on me. Miss Ready For Whatever and Leave Ya In a Moment had become Miss Whateva You Like Sir. My family could not believe it and my close friends could not get over it. However, I believed in family and I wanted my children to have a father and mother who were together.

When Kenneth and I decided to get married, my mother did not approve. It was just me and him at the chapel and we used someone from a different wedding party to be our witness. We both worked, but I could not keep a job long because I was always accused of sleeping with co-workers and managers. He called so much to one job and always held me up to make me late that I was released from my duties. I had excellent job evaluations and the company ended up paying me for all vacation and sick time I would have earned. A major corporation too. Looking back on it now, I wonder if they really knew what I was going through due to my actions or tear stained face.

    Well, that money became part of our moving money. His job wanted him to transfer out of state. He probably asked for it. He was jealous of the relationship I had with my mother and wanted us separated. He wanted me to have no one but him. I was to breathe, dream, and think of only him.

    To be continued............

***

Bound by Chains will be available soon – be sure to purchase this remarkable story of strength and courage.

Although it has been years and Nikki is no longer with Kenneth, as one can tell her wounds are still healing.

Allow them to heal baby sis. I am proud of you.

You truly are a remarkable woman!!!